WAR REPORTER

Dan O'Brien is an American playwright and poet living in Los Angeles. His play *The Body of an American* premiered in 2012 and was the inaugural winner of the Edward M. Kennedy Prize for Drama.

'*War Reporter* is a book-length sequence of poems that anyone interested in the fate of American poetry should read, even must read. As Wallace Stevens once wrote, poetry has to "think about war / And it has to find what will suffice." Dan O'Brien knows this in his bones. He has dug into American history, into our perpetual war, and found sufficient words – words that meet the people of his time with language adequate to their experience. I can't speak highly enough of these poems. The book is superb, subtle, memorable, and of a piece.' – JAY PARINI

'Dan O'Brien has discovered the poetry in the most harrowing of war stories, and made music of the ways in which we share in each other's guilts, doubts, and triumphs. Meanwhile, the poet's identity bleeds into that of war reporter, photographer, and reader. This is a tragic book about the human comedy.' – MARY-JO SALTER

'The complex, disquieting truth of war as both lure and destroyer binds together poet and journalist. The result is a memorable book.' – ANTHONY FEINSTEIN, author of *Journalists Under Fire: The Psychological Hazards of Covering War*

WAR REPORTER
Dan O'Brien

First published in 2013
by CB editions
146 Percy Road London W12 9QL
www.cbeditions.com

Printed in England by Blissetts, London W3 8DH

ISBN 978–0–9573266–7–5

Call war damnable – there is nothing too bad that can be said about it – and yet, it has a knack, which peace never learned, of uncovering the splendor in commonplace persons.

– *The Love of an Unknown Soldier: found in a dugout*, 1918

Acknowledgements

Many of these poems have been previously printed in the following magazines: *5 AM, Arroyo Literary Review, Bayou Magazine, Birmingham Poetry Review, Charition Review, Clackamas Review, Cold Mountain Review, Cossack Review, Cyphers, Event, Grain Magazine, Greensboro Review, Hanging Loose, Kelsey Review, Knockout Magazine, Linebreak, Magma Poetry, Malahat Review, Mississippi Review, Missouri Review, The Moth, North American Review, The Owls, Permafrost, Poetry Review, Saint Anne's Review, Screech Owl, South Carolina Review, storySouth, St Petersburg Review, Sugar House Review, Tampa Review, Tears in the Fence, Two Weeks (Linebreak* anthology), *upstreet, War, Literature & the Arts, The White Review, ZYZZYVA.*

Paul Watson has been a war reporter for more than two decades. He is best known, perhaps, for his 1994 Pulitzer Prize-winning photo of the body of an American soldier dragged from the wreck of a Black Hawk through the streets of Mogadishu. When Paul took this picture he heard the dead man speak to him: 'If you do this, I will own you forever.'

These poems are derived from Paul's memoir *Where War Lives*, his journalism, recordings and transcripts and, most valuably to me, our emails and conversations. Some of the poems take place in Ulukhaktok in the Canadian High Arctic, where I visited Paul in the winter of 2010 while he was enjoying a hiatus from war reporting, covering the 'Arctic and Aboriginal Beat' for the *Toronto Star*. He has since gone back to covering Kandahar and other, more recent war zones.

Several years ago my birth family disintegrated for bewildering, mysterious reasons. That I discovered Paul's work around the same time wasn't a coincidence. Early in our correspondence Paul sent me something I'll paraphrase: 'Do you know that quote of Camus' where he says he's solved the mystery of where war lives? It lives in each of us. In the loneliness and humiliation we all feel. If we can solve that conflict within ourselves then maybe we'll be able to rid the world of war.' Paul's writing, and mine in response, are as much about our private, internal wars as they are about the constantly roving holocaust of modern warfare.

D. O'B.
April 21, 2013
Los Angeles

Contents

WAR REPORTER

The War Reporter Paul Watson Hears the Voice

We ask them, Have you seen the American
soldier? Someone says he saw him tied up
in a wheelbarrow. I take a picture
of children bouncing on a rotor blade
in the smoldering wreckage of a Black Hawk.
Has anyone seen the dead American
soldier? The mob parts around me, I look
down in the street. And I meet the man. When
you take a picture the camera covers
your face, you shut the rest of the world out,
everything goes dim. And I hear a voice
both in my head and out. *If you do this,*
I will own you forever. I'm sorry
but I have to. *If you do this, I will*
own you. I'm sorry, I'm not trying to
desecrate your memory. If you do this
I will own you forever. I took his
picture. While they were beating his body
and cheering. Some spitting. Some kid wearing
a chopper crewman's goggles, face screwed up
in rapturous glee while giving the dead man
the finger. An old man's raising his cane
like a club and thudding it down against
the dead flesh. Men holding the ropes that bind
the dead man's wrists are stretching his arms out
over his head, rolling him back and forth
in the hammering morning light. I'm standing
outside myself. I'm watching someone else
take these pictures. Wondering, You poor man.
Who are you?

The War Reporter Paul Watson Prepares for His Next Trip

Reading glasses, check. Sensible shoes, check.
Endless tangles of cords. When I was born
I had these nubbins instead of fingers
till the doctor snipped them off. The hand is
attached to a wrist that bends, with a palm
as big as an infant's. In Kosovo
they used to think I was a wounded vet
and give me all kinds of free shit. iPod,
check. Satphone, laptop, checks. Bars of anti
-microbial soap. There's a thunderstorm and
my son's asleep. Today he asked me, When
you're dead will you still watch us? Recently
on a riverboat in the Irrawaddy
Delta, one of the thousands of corpses
floating in the paddies is the body
of a child. In pajama bottoms with
teddy bear cartoons on it. The bleached skin's
like rotting rattan. The leg bones yellow.
The stench is unbearable, but the people
on shore don't seem to care. My fixer says
that as Buddhists they believe the body
is nothing more than an empty vessel,
and the soul has already been reborn
as someone new. After several stiff drinks
that night I lay on the roof of our boat
staring up into the stars, imagining
I was nothing more than a passenger
on this rotting vessel, my body. Pills,
estimate time away then multiply
by eleven a day for depression,
hypertension, polycystic kidney

disease. Toss in a few extra in case
I get kidnapped. The lightning is lighting
up my son's sleeping face. Leaning in close
I whisper, Don't be afraid. I'll come back
home soon. Do not be afraid. Japanese
green tea for antioxidants, corkscrew
for the cheap Bordeaux I'll purchase en route
at Duty Free, more antioxidants and
some liquid courage to help ease the pain
of these five-star hotel room blues.

The War Reporter Paul Watson on Winning the Pulitzer Prize

Then somehow I find myself in a room
like the Pantheon and the Parthenon
confused. Wide gleaming chevrons of cold cuts
fanned out on aproned tables. Wearing shoes
and a navy blazer, wool slacks picked out
just this morning at Brooks Brothers. My boss
eyes me. *I guess I feel guilty about*
that dead soldier's family. Kevin Carter,
who only last month was snorting Ritalin
off the floor of my apartment before
blasting into the townships, wins also
for his picture of a vulture waiting
implacably for a skeletal child
to stop struggling to lift her swollen head
from the blood-red clay. Like Carter waited
for that vulture to unfold its sere wings
which it never did, which gives his picture
such leaden, boring doom. *Do you hear that*
applause, Watson? They love us! Months later
I'm back in Rwanda documenting
machete mouths in the legs of women
who'd hid waist-deep in mud. My satellite
phone relays a message. *Kevin Carter*
took his own life. Duct-taped a garden hose
to his exhaust pipe. Left a suicide note
that I'll paraphrase. *I have been haunted*
so now I will haunt you. With my eyes closed
I see him waiting in the shade ashing
his cigarette onto his lens. Waiting
for the vulture's promised embrace. Waiting
for the good shot.

The War Reporter Paul Watson on Suicide

On a bed we discover the body
of a child at the bottom of a pile
of children. Quartered like chickens. Outside
another's buried alive. The hand is
like a tuber. At the refugee camp
a girl stumbles barefoot into a ditch
of corpses. Some wrapped in reed mats. Looking
for help, crying. But nobody's coming.
I say to myself, This will make a great
picture. This is a beautiful picture
somehow. Raising my camera to my face
I step on a dead old woman's arm: it
snaps like a stick. In Nyarubuye
we push open a gate on a courtyard
of Hell. Tangles of limbs junked. They'd come to
this church hoping God would protect them but
it only made things that much easier
to be hacked to pieces. A survivor
shivers on the filthy foam. The mayor
asked for wallets, tossed them grenades. Men blown
into pieces in midair. *These are snakes*
whose heads must be crushed. Neighbors took neighbors'
children and bashed their heads together till
brains strewed the dirt. Infants keening beside
their decapitated mothers were plunged
head-first into latrines. A pregnant friend
slit open and her fetus extruded
like a docile calf. There was so much noise!
the survivor recalls. All I wanted
was to close my ears and lay on the ground
and sleep in my family's blood. Till her skin

7

itched with maggots. Then 40 days cowering
in the charnel church. Praying I'd be killed
too because I believed the world had been
swept away. *Of course I've wanted to kill
myself before*, writes the war reporter
to the poet, but the truth is I lack
the courage. So I tell myself, Just go
someplace dangerous, let somebody else
kill you.

The Poet Hears the Voice

In Princeton the leaves change like bells. Squirrels
pass untouchable girls. Stalking the greens
at night. Worth something. Running in lightning
storms, peeling paint from balusters along
the Victorian porch. Sipping vodka
neat, cooking meat over charcoal. Watching
the unified mind of the swallows come
careering out of the twilight into
our backyard maple tree. *I tend to be
solitary. Dinner parties, I prefer
to stay away.* This is you speaking though
it might as well be me. *I've spent my life
with war reporters, and I'll count myself
foremost in this group: everyone's a mess
of insecurities, looking for self
-esteem through risk.* A hangar-sized Whole Foods
beside a glinting field of Priuses,
while you're off in Kandahar or is it
Baghdad, Paul? *I'm sick of being lied to,
so I simply take it as a challenge
to find the truth.* My father cursing me:
There are things you do not know. My mother
not turning her mausolean face to say
goodbye. Picking up our lives at the end
of summer, I swear I heard a demon
hiss, Don't leave us, please. *If something's risky
and we probably shouldn't do it I'll say,
Don't worry about me, I'm already
dead.* The blind mob is calling, You poor man,
who are you?

Portrait of the War Reporter Paul Watson as a Young Man

I was in a band called Eruption, we
did a shitload of drugs: California
Sunshine, Purple Microdot, Windowpane.
My best friend Richard and I listening
to *Dark Side of the Moon* in the middle
of a circle we'd burnt into a field
behind my house. Electrical towers
arcing overhead. Richard got me hooked
on Albert Camus, Nietzsche. We'd chew some
peyote before gym class and get off
on the psychedelic rainbows trailing
behind high jumpers and kids doing flips
off balance beams. Oh, and our friend Andy
blew his fucking brains out at his parents'
lake cottage. It was hardly a surprise,
he was stuck outside himself. I hung out
with this dealer? he must've been 30.
At a motel he pulls out a bottle
and a baggie full of pills. Up or down,
my choice. I wash down a few with a belt
of whiskey. An hour later he's carving
his arm with his knife. *Bitches always want
perfection!* Then he's slinging my body
over his back like I'm some medevaced
grunt on TV in Vietnam. Dumping
me in a taxi. Puking through a chain
-link fence in the middle of a vacant
lot as the taxi spits dirt. My teacher
took us on a field trip to Algonquin
Provincial Park once. Under a mystery
of stars. With my classmate Stephen Harper,

future Prime Minister of Canada,
no shit, behind me paddling. Thinking, Who
could not love Albert Camus? And that's how
I ended up winning the Pulitzer
Prize.

The War Reporter Paul Watson Imagines His Father

He's liberating a medieval city
in France, twisted streets, churches and houses
made of stone. My father takes a bullet
in his thigh. He watches one of his men
trapped in the long grass. Each time the man moves
a Nazi shoots him. He can't do a thing
but watch this man die. Each time the friend cries out
for help, when he moves again, he gets shot
till he's dead. My mother and my father
ride a streetcar. A manhole cover pops
and he's gone. She gets off at the next stop
and walks home, sits down on the front stoop and
waits all day for my father to return.
Once in a while my brother would remove
the Luger from the dead man's closet. Once
he let me hold it and I imagined
I was the man who pulled the trigger like
I take my pictures now.

The War Reporter Paul Watson Was Talking to His Mother

and I asked her, Did you ever ask him
about what happens after? He'd been sick
for a while, of the same kidney disease
that's killing me. Did my father believe
he'd be going somewhere? And she said, Well
how should I know? Ha ha ha. We just talked
about, you know, how to take care of all
you kids, what our savings account was and
that sort of thing. And I told her, You know,
I find that hard to believe. He's staring
into the abyss – how could he face this
fact? And she just shrugged and answered, Bravely,
I suppose. And, well, that kind of told me
everything I need to know.

The War Reporter Paul Watson's South African Psychiatrist Tells a Story

I'm sitting in an Eames chair. I'm scribbling
on a legal pad. But when I was fresh
out of medical school they sent us away
to the border. With headlines proclaiming,
We are *not* in Angola! Hours later
you're flying, red incandescent floating
flares like angels in the trees. Descending
towards the white soldiers. Left with nothing
but my knife and my pistol. Sunbathing
on our stretchers, listening to our Walkmen,
when you hear a mine explode a cougar
will be dinner. Daubing bug bites all day,
riding by night through the thorn brush hunting
the Black Threat. When you get killed your family
will only be informed you've disappeared
along a border that doesn't exist.

The War Reporter Paul Watson's Psychiatrist Takes Note

Patient is punctual. In freefall. Tells me
he's more likely to believe in ghosts than
psychology. He shivers. Insisting
he's never been in love, when he is. Who
will take him home today? He prefers to
keep things simple. Overwhelming hunger
to be dead, disturbed about unfairness
in politics. Do you think your deformed
hand's related to this never-ending
strain to catch the banner? Patient laughs. Wracked
with guilt about a martyred mother. Sibs
single, blank stare why. Sisters especially
seething with envy. So he medicates
himself with booze, marijuana. His mood is
swinging, dizzied and nauseated from
the SSRIs. Patient informs me
he's leaving our country for good. Zaire
en route to Rwanda's maelstrom. Cut up
over losing the love of the insane
woman who torments him. He cries. A short
and broken therapy. Didn't happen
at all the way these things should.

The War Reporter Paul Watson Describes the Ghost

This is who I've always been. My mind is
simply speaking to itself. *Is he here
with us now?* He's always with us, whispering,
This can not last. And of course he laments
whenever I lift the blade away from
my skin. I don't believe, you know, a ghost
could come walking through that door with his shroud
streaming clouds of what-have-you. I believe
there's a price to pay for everything. Words
fail. But in the end everybody knows
not to desecrate the dead. That mob knows
what they did. And I can only hope that
they're haunted like I am by the Afghan
looter raising his mortar barrel to
my camera. *If I'm honest I'm afraid
of meeting you, Paul!* You're like the writer
I've always wished I were. This mythical
figure with your withered hand, your constant
returning to an underworld we can't
look at, or won't look at. An Iraqi
looter's wedding his mortar barrel with
my laptop. *And immediately the heat
was on President Clinton to decide
what to do.* And that decision was to
run away. So when 800,000
Tutsi got dismembered in Rwanda
in a hundred days, Clinton kept quiet
for four more years before he said the word
genocide. And we all know Al-Qaeda
was in Somalia back then. It says so
on indictments in US Federal Court,

bin Laden's bragged about it, his minions
brag about it. I think it's safe to say
take everything that happened but remove
my picture, and Al-Qaeda would not have
chased us out of Somalia, bin Laden
would not have been able to proclaim, See,
we're able to do this! we need only
small victories to defeat history's greatest
military. Enter my photograph
and it's 9/11, and this never
-ending war on terror. *It's true the ghost
has gotten quieter, Dan, like he's biding
his time.* Like in a slasher film. My son
will die from leukemia, or get burnt up
with my wife in a wreck. Who gives a shit
about me? I know everyone enjoys
a good ghost story, but it rarely works
that way. You get more used to it, it turns
into someone else's problem.

The Poet Waits for the War Reporter Paul Watson to Reply

Wisconsin in winter. This visiting
professor's entombed in a renovated
schoolhouse. Researching spirits. When I hear
a girl laugh, then footsteps. My wife back home
is having trouble with her brain. The gland
in my neck aches. Let's Google it. Let's Skype,
do you want to Skype, Paul? Through my window
a freight train earthquakes past, its bell tolling
over and over as the traffic wicks
under the blinking red light and the snow
accretes on Lake Monona, covering
the sign Obama stuck in the ice: *Yes
We Can!* Spring Break. Two people are murdered
down the street. A man my age and a girl
within the month. Both stabbed repeatedly
in the afternoon at home. I'm running
on the glowing ice past rain-stained faces
on telephone poles. Just like I used to
race past the makeshift morgue outside Bellevue
that recent September. My father? He
was always home. He never talked unless
it was to tell you how fucking stupid
you were. Why aren't you answering these
emails, Paul? Where are you now? That freight train's
approaching fast, its headlamp swallowing
a tunnel of snow. The chiming bell and
the haunting horn.

The War Reporter Paul Watson on Guilt

This was in Mosul at the beginning
of the war. A boy was throwing pebbles
at a machine gun twisting like a hose
spraying death. A bunch of students pulling
another student bleeding from a gash
over his eyes. Someone made that sound *click*
like, you know, Take his picture! I had to
swap my lenses, and you could see the switch
go off in someone's head. I was lifted
off the ground, tossed around, stoned. Someone slid
his knife into my back and I could feel
the blood pool in my shirt. I was trying
to hold on to my camera as they stretched
my arms out like this till I was floating
on top of the mob, and I'm not trying
to be cinematic but it was like
Christ on the cross. *I am not innocent*
nor have I ever been. I don't deserve
your mercy. But the truth of these places
is always the same. A dozen people
formed a circle around me, a dozen
people against a thousand. Approaching
a row of shuttering shops. And these people
simply pulled the shutters back up and shoved
me under. That's when I saw my camera's
gone, the hand's empty, the mob is pounding
on metal. The tea shop owner says, Look
you know I'd really like to help you but
would you mind leaving my tea shop soon? Out
into the street again lying prostrate
in the dust at the order of some pissed

-off marines, and somehow I convinced them
to take me back behind the wire. That's why
I can't blame it all on my brain, Dan. Or
my father dying when I was young. Or
this missing hand. It would be poetic
justice to get ripped apart. Remember
what the ghost promised me: *If you do this
I will own you.* I just have this feeling
he's thinking, *You watched my desecration,
now here comes yours.*

The War Reporter Paul Watson on Love

Getting high together on a bridge while
Rwandan refugees spilled out across
the border. Rwandan corpses spilled out
over the waterfall and down into
the whirlpool. Khareen loved rococo art,
homemade knödles and beer for dinner. Once
she sat on her father's lap with her arm
around his neck, like this. Another time
she flashed her tits at me down the hallway
in her father's condo. I don't know why
I feel the need to keep mentioning her
father. She was blonde. Great body. Sexy
voice. Called me Paulie. We shared a house but
I paid the rent. I lived in a closet
-sized room off the kitchen. I was happiest
on her leash, so to speak. I'd sit with her
while she was taking a bath or lying
in bed with candles lit, while she got off
beneath the covers. It's not sex, she'd say,
it's just for comfort. Once she let this guy
into our yard to watch through the window
while she fucked this other guy. She told me
this at breakfast, in detail. She wanted
to be a war reporter, so we went
to Rwanda where we met this handsome
aid worker named Laurent. Building latrines
for refugees. While I'm shooting pictures
with my one hand. That night she was lying
in his cot, under his netting, scribbling
in her diary. So Laurent got a room
in our hotel. With grenades exploding

in the shanties and the death squads spreading
through the streets, I call downstairs. She answers
laughing, Paulie? Let's go, Khareen. Stop that,
Laurent! They're killing people outside. Don't
touch me, Laurent! He moved into the house
with us when we came home. They'd fight then fuck
like teenagers. When I broke up with her
she howled like her throat had been slit, climbing
onto the balcony railing. Hong Kong
below that whirlpool again. How could I
ever think I'd get away with this?

The War Reporter Paul Watson Lost His Camera

Vacationing in Cape Town, longing to purge
yourself with Stellenbosch and lobster. Waves
lash the scapular limestone. Unshouldering
your camera on your molt of clothes you dip
into the bay while it sways till you might
let yourself get carried away. Onshore
a baboon. A dog's trot. His ponytail
-like tail sweeping the coral wash. Fumbling
your camera with spidery paws, weighing
your self in his scales. Found wanting. Champing
canines into the salt-stained strap he climbs
into the thorny strandveld. Where a breeze
bothers his pelt as he squats like a thug
-gish Buddha. Jaundiced eyes and gun muzzle
-like muzzle daring you. To holler. Hurl
skipping stones from the sliding tide. He ducks
behind a tree. And here comes your camera
sailing the daylit half-moon, exploding
off the exposed, foam-flecked table, spewing
guts that had fixed the souls of so many
undone by man. Baring your fangs you howl
your thanks as much as your dread. But it's just
a camera. Remember.

The War Reporter Paul Watson Has Dinner with Aideed

Black men in thongs and sarongs flung grenades
at white-faced soldiers dangling from the womb
of that laboring Black Hawk. Shit and garbage
clouds enveloped the bird. One lucky shot
made of her tail blade a sparrow. Shrieking
metal scarified alley walls. At dawn
a girl smiled at me while swinging her string
of particolored flesh on a stick. Hags
unwrapped his molar from a scrap of blood
-mottled newsprint. *America! America!*
as a migraine throb. The headless torso
of another wheeled away for display
at Bakara Market, where useless notes
purchased a burlesque inside the burlap
mess. *Nest of flies, net of blood.* All because
we'd caught The Thin One, this bagman who'd taught
the even thinner ones to modify
Ethiopian hand grenades to detonate
at the apex of their arcs. *Satellite
dishes on The Thin One's roof. Shattered glass
groaning underfoot.* A prowling Jaguar
panting at the gate. Hottentot hookers
stacked in back like bales of hay burying
our needle Aideed. Teens in Adidas
T-shirts cocked their chambers. I turned my back
counting each breath until the end. After
The Picture. After America had sunk
back into the floodplain, Aideed sent me
his invitation. *He wants to thank you
for all that you've done.* My fixer's grinning
Death's head in the doorway. Decorative drapes

drawn at the safe house. A frayed wire running
to a low-wattage bulb. When fatherly
Aideed unfolded his arms I allowed
myself to be embraced as a son might
survive incest. Prisoner for the evening
to this satyr gloating over his goat
stew spewed on canjeero bread. The common
plate, slick fingers mingling. I asked him, Sir,
was that you I saw weeks ago outside
The Thin One's house? The psychopath revealed
childlike teeth. *I came to help the people,*
I came to calm them down. I came to save
us from ourselves.

The War Reporter Paul Watson on Censorship

Car door's shut. Engine's idling. The mob is
muffled. Out of Somalia and into
a wobbling canoe years ago in
Sudan. Drifting downriver at sunset
with Andrew Stawicki, Polish émigré
photographer who snaps a picture of
boys running naked like a snake along
the river's bloody spine. That's going to be
a beautiful picture. They won't print it.
Why not? The kid's dick is showing! *Open
the door! Open it!* This time I frame out
everything shameful. Except the woman
slapping the corpse with a flattened tin can
and the boy shoveling his face through the mob
to laugh at us.

The Poet Runs

from LA at sunset. Women's faces
are slick masks thanks to Botox. Some men look
embalmed and tan also. Helicopters
over Brentwood like they're still looking for
OJ's white Bronco. Or for rioting blacks
and browns in South Central. While I'm soldiering
up Amalfi to Sunset the Palisades
look more like the hills of South Korea
on *MASH*. Or Tuscany. While you're somewhere
in Kandahar. I've filled my prescription
for Zoloft, Paul. I'm enjoying living
in my strange new home. Along the margin
of the ocean upsetting a conclave
of gulls into whole shoals lifting. Hot girls
watching the sun set. *Who is that running*
with me? a shadow, over my shoulder
in the sun and sand. Like my brother or
some other fallen angel. Shackleton
staggering through the blizzard with his comrades
starving, delirious. How they kept seeing
a fourth with them. How they kept asking, Who
is that fourth who walks always beside you?
and Eliot put that in his *Waste Land* but
revised four into three for poetic
reasons. On the horizon sand plovers
bundling like a haze of corpseflies before
the satiate smudge of fire. The rolling foam
of breaking waves is suddenly sublime
ice floes. Is the man running after me
the man who haunts you? And what could he want
from me?

When will we ever meet? I've got to go
to the Philippines where Abu Sayyaf
the neighborhood Al-Qaeda affiliate
is on the march once more. I'm worried that
my editor, who hates me for reasons
I can't even begin to imagine,
won't like it. It's not the sort of story
that tends to garner those coveted clicks
on the *LA Times* website. Here's a link
to a soundbite directly from the mouth
of our paper's reptilian overlord
Sam Zell: http://gawker.com/
5002815/exclusive
-sam-zell-says-fuck-you-to-his-journalist
– *My attitude on journalism is
simply: I want to make enough money
so I can afford you!* Now while it's true
I like a gutter-talking millionaire
as much as the next guy, I do wonder
what he's up to? Especially after
publishing a new employee manual
telling us all to "question authority"
and "push back." *I'm sorry, I'm sorry but
you're giving me the classic what I call
journalistic arrogance of deciding
that puppies do not count!* With the chaos
building at the gates in Afghanistan
and Iraq, he's just the sort of leader
I don't want to get killed for. *Hopefully
we'll get to the point where our revenue
is so significant we'll be able*

to do both puppies and Iraq. Okay?
– *Fuck you!* Don't you think it's kind of strange, Paul,
that you've never heard my voice? I've heard yours
in this series of tubes known as the World
Wide Web. Let's set this trip up now! I won
a grant to come see you. *Congratulations
on the grant!* I've got a rusted RV
in Bali, we can watch the surf and drink
and talk genocide. Only problem is
I finally got laid off. And my RV
just got crushed by a tree. But have no fear!
I've got an idea. *My wife's an actress
on a TV show that flops.* Everyone
assumes we're sad, but we're not. It's winter
but it's sunny and warm. Every season
is sunny and warm. I can't remember
what year it is without thinking. The days
get shorter or longer but the sun stays
the same. It's beautiful. It's beautiful.
It's beautiful. *I'm going to move back home
to Canada, where word is I'll cover
the Arctic aboriginal beat.* Shooting
pictures, writing stories, blogging about
life in the midnight sun. Or the noontime
moon. In any case I've been waking up
thankful each morning I won't have to write
another sentence about Al-Qaeda
ever again. Unless bin Laden's found
in an ice cave somewhere. *You have no clue
how happy this makes me, Paul!* How could you
know how much the ice and snow and howling

wind speak to me? Much more so than the sun
of LA or Bali. Trapped in pack ice
for months, sometimes years. Scurvy, insanity,
cannibalism. It helps me relax
and fall asleep. Maybe I could visit
you there this winter? *Why won't you tell me*
something true, Dan? Something that makes you feel
as embarrassed as I've felt telling you
all this. Do you know that quote of Camus'
where he says that war lives in each of us?
and if we can only solve the conflict
within ourselves – then we'll be able to
end all war. What do you think? Are you shocked
I'm hopeful at all? *My brother walking*
out from under the trees with his body
white with snow. No jacket. Barefoot. He'd jumped
from a window and fallen three stories
without breaking a bone. That night atop
the staircase to the attic, Mother cried
in my arms. Whispering, This is a secret
we will take to our graves. I felt compelled
to wash the blood from my hands. Scrupulous
in word and deed and thought. I was afraid
of doorknobs. And thereby found poetry. Till
a lifetime later I'm getting married
and my father tells me I'll slit my throat
soon. Screaming, Just like your brother! Or his
brother, who'd disappeared not long after
I was born. You are the spitting image
of this man. There are things you do not know!
my mother and my father could not stop

shouting together. I understood how
it was they were still in love. There are things
you do not know! So I sit at my desk
clicking on a button that shows me where
in the world everyone is who visits
my website. And believe me not many
people do. When I said I never hear
from my family, that's not true. I can tell
my mother's on my website at least once
a day. Sometimes twice. It's a compulsion
I know, but still I like seeing these dots
on the map. But it's nothing! it's nothing
to complain about. It's the sort of thing
everybody has. And nothing compared
to the unspeakable acts of cruelty
you've seen, Paul. *Let's meet up in the Arctic
in 24-hour darkness, Dan.* Hotels
there are like dorms for racist construction
workers from the south, and the costs run high
since everything's flown in. But the ambience
will be just perfect. So let me know when
you'd like to come, and I'll put together
some kind of plan.

The Poet Takes Flight

LAX to Vancouver, Vancouver
to Yellowknife. What the hell kind of name
is Yellowknife? I read how the copper
in the drumlins turns the Inuits' knives
that color. Yellowknife to Kugluktuk
by twin turboprop. How do you say that
name again? Kugluktuk. But I don't know
Inuktitut. What's that? Their language. Whose?
The Inuit. Which means simply people
in Inuktitut. I'm getting all this
information off Wikipedia
on my new iTouch. The flight attendant's
an Inuit kid. Gay, goth, nose ring and
an attitude. *Does anybody want
this last bottle of water?* A black guy
named Isaac shares the aisle with me. *You done
with that paper, mon? Listen: Beyoncé
says even though she isn't from the hood
she understands the struggles of the hood,
ha ha ha!* An old Inuit woman
wearing an anorak like calico
fringed with coyote fur, and a wide hood
obscuring everything but her mouth, says
nothing to us. A girl with an iPod
smudges her window towards a cluster
of buried houses. *We have cell phones now
also.* Grandma and the iPod shuffling
across the burnt ice plain of Kugluktuk
while Isaac and I fly two more hours north
to Ulukhaktok. Where the airport is
a room, the cab's a van gliding across

a desert of ice. The cabbie's a hick
from Newfoundland. *You teaching basketball
eh?* No, soccer mon. *That'll be twenty
dollars flat, eh.* I got it, I got it
– Welcome to the North, my mon! The hotel's
a prefabricated house, corrugated
tin roof for maybe six windows. Clorox
and electric baseboard heat. Babushka
-like women flipping burgers. *Are you Dan?
I'm Paul.* His hair's messed up. He needs a shave.
His thick wool socks are sloughing off. Pink eyes
with dilated pupils. Who is he? Who
does this remind me of? The demoniac
in the tombs. Who's broken every shackle
and the fetters off his feet. Not a man
strong enough to subdue him. Night and day
bruising himself with stones. Howling across
the vast, impenetrable wastes. His hand's
not there. But he's got a kind of a thumb
rubbing his clenched brow as we speak. Don't look,
Dan. Not now. Show what kind of man you are
by not noticing him. And I wonder
what he sees in me? *Hey, I like your beard
and hair. Has anyone ever told you
you look a bit like Jesus?*

The War Reporter Paul Watson and the Poet Go for a Walk in the Arctic

Blood is scattered like what it is, or jewels
around the body of a seal. Belly
-up, frozen whiskers, mostly canine snout.
Its abdomen is open to the wind
like a broken birdcage. Steam rising up.
The Inuit hunter's untangling guts
like a bunch of udon noodles. Squeezing
the weedy shit onto the ice, slicing
out the beet red organs neatly, flopping
them into a plastic tray on the boot
of his skidoo. They're good stuff when they're cooked,
he says. Stomach, heart. My boys just love it
when my wife cooks these! Paul asks for a piece
of liver. Sliding it off the wide blade
of the hunter's knife, Tastes like sushi! When
I ask him if he misses Iraq and
places like that, he answers, My body's
been craving raw meat.

The War Reporter Paul Watson Pays the Poet
a Compliment

Two strangers emerging from the Arctic
ice. Into the cozy horn of smoke-plumed
slums. The older one shouldering the camera
asks, *How do you do what you do?* Some days
I can barely lift the phone to my face
for a story. My arms quake, voice shakes. See
that lone figure gaining on us like Death
out of the setting noonday sun? across
this shortcut of the frozen bay? That's Rex
the Inuit sculptor. He carves outside
in the wind so granite flecks will flurry
away from his lungs. I interviewed him
yesterday, and now he walks right past me
without saying a word! Maybe I should
have bought a walrus tusk off him. *Stumbling
like a revenant or an alcoholic
up the driven, alabaster shore. Past
the grounded schooner that used to ferry
his kids to school.* I really don't know how
you can spend your life in a room speaking
to nobody. If only I could live
without paychecks, pensions, health insurance
and remove myself from the world and write
something about myself, for myself – that
would take some real courage. But that's something
I'll never do. *Two strangers emerging
from the Arctic ice. The stupid one asks,*
Why can't you?

The War Reporter Paul Watson and the Poet Try to Have Fun

with the usual boys of summer shooting
slapshots like rifles. Puck-scuffed Plexiglas
rebounding off Paul's gaze. The Somalian
kid in the chopper crewman's goggles grins
at us. The top of another boy's head's
been sliced open like an egg, his skull wiped
clean inside by bullet fire. The infant's
head twists off its chest, topples from the bed
to the warped wood floor. Sand is snow. Let's go
okay? This lighting's for shit and these damn
kids keep knocking my camera. *How many*
hands you have? I have two, you have two but
what happened to Paul? Oh well, he was born
that way. Just like you were born Inuit
and I was born with anxiety. *Help him!*
Help him! Why won't you help your friend? See that
hole in the wall, Dan? Most people notice
that and think someone's been drilling. I see
a bullet hole. How fucked is that? Fording
flumes of snow indistinguishable from
celestial dunes. Wondering who is that man
following us? *Why don't we try to find*
a shaman, Paul? I've read the Inuit
still believe that shamans can turn themselves
into animals, seals and bears. Into
other people too. All in the pursuit
of exorcising ghosts. An Arctic hare
like a newborn standing weirdly upright
in the skidoo's sweeping glare. When the light's
gone, hare's gone also. Oh, which reminds me,
Dan, I'm trying to set up a sled ride

with these Inuit hunters. 500
dollars but I'll pay it, or the *Star* will
I mean. While flakes of snow drift down like dust
off the high shelf. Wasted men in doorways
let us pass. Graffiti warning, *Arctic*
for life! Because the Internet's calling
for snow tonight, but we'll try to have fun
tomorrow if the weather's any good.

The War Reporter Paul Watson Watches TV

I guess I just like watching sports, hockey
and football mostly. Entertainment news
cause I like to watch beautiful people
do stupid things. It calms me down. I love
hearing the women's curling team screaming,
Harder! Faster! All these girls with their brooms
rubbing a path in the ice for the weight
or the pot or kettle or whatever
it's called, screaming, Harder! Faster! As if
that does anything, really! What about
The Bachelor? Have you seen *The Bachelor*? Look,
she's pretending to cry. She's pretending
to cry! What are all these people, actors?
Strippers? She's trying so damn hard to cry
real tears! Harder! Faster! How's it looking
out there? *Who can tell if snow is falling*
out of the sky or up from a treeless
lunarscape? Do you want another glass
of Margaux? This your mug? When I'm calling
my brothers and sisters and they're whining
about problems at work, I like to say,
How long we been talking? Fifteen minutes.
I say, Now you're fifteen minutes closer
to death. Cause it bugs me to the core how
people don't notice how quickly we die
driving to work, tanning on a beach in
Phuket and this wave comes out of nowhere
and just keeps coming. Unmute this. I love
this movie. Look at those legs! Meryl Streep
is on the run or she's on the river
actually, ha ha ha, in a rafting

boat trying to escape from this psycho
-killer Kevin Bacon. Is this movie
good? or shit? It's shit. But God Meryl Streep
is so gorgeous.

The War Reporter Paul Watson on War Reporting

In the beginning it was just because
I felt insecure. I'm sure you used to
feel that way too, Dan. I wanted people
to say I was brave, and heroic. Then
I grew to hate it but I still needed
that fix of adrenalin. Where I am
today? I don't need it. But now I see
the other reporters doing my job
just don't get it. Or if they do get it
there's no way they're going to tell it because
they want a seat at the Sunday morning
round table. They want their own show. They want
a bank of studio lights powered by
generators outside the embassy.
I just want to chip away at the lies
now. But that's a losing game. Most people
don't care what's going on, or they don't know
what they're supposed to do. The phosphorous
bombs dropping on Fallujah in '04
that melted the skin off children. I could
go on and on and on and on. I see
it like a labyrinth. If you get the truth
you get out. But you don't, it just gets worse,
you get more lost. And the harder you try
the darker it gets. As opposed to what,
being like you, I suppose. Right? Who cares?
Let's watch some more TV. Let's drink more wine.
As long as I'm safe I don't need to do
a thing. You see, this is why I don't talk
to anyone. People ask me questions
they don't want the answers to.

The War Reporter Paul Watson on God

See, bin Laden is bin Laden because
he never had enough love. And George Bush
is George Bush because nobody loved him
enough. John Lennon was right, and Mother
Theresa was right. Mohammad. I love
my wife dearly, but there are moments when
my love becomes pure like when I'm lying
in my bed in a hotel and outside
every pulse of light, every detonation
means another hundred dead. And I'm not
afraid anymore. I have been taken
into the center of the beating heart
of God. I mean I don't really believe
in Him. I honestly can't imagine
He'd let all this happen. I have no clue
if there's an afterlife or what my role
in this life should be. But there is something
we don't understand yet. Some things happen
for a reason. Which is why I wrote you
back a few years ago when you wrote me
for no reason. But there was a reason,
right?

The War Reporter Paul Watson Telexes from the New War

VARIOUS SPANISH ARE HOLDING ON AND OH
I SHOULD ADD A FINE YOUNG IRISH LASSIE
BILL. HOLD ON PAUL UPSTAIRS IS ORDERING YOU
OUT IN THE MORNING BUT GOOD LUCK TONIGHT
WITH THAT FIERY PIECE O'TAIL ARE YOU STILL
THERE COULD SOMEONE PLEASE CALL PAUL WATSON BACK
TO THE MACHINE? 426138
TSTAR SA HELLO BILL ANYONE
AWAKE OVER THERE? OF COURSE WE'RE AWAKE
WE WORK FOR A LIVING. PEOPLE RUNNING
THROUGH LOBBY FEAR COULD BE REAL THING ASSUME
BOMBS ARE DROPPING. ARE THERE BOMBS DROPPING NOW
OR NOT? I DON'T KNOW. HAS THE WAR STARTED
YET OR NOT PAUL? I DON'T KNOW LIGHTS OUT AIR
SIRENS MEN SCREAMING WOMEN CRYING PLEASE
ADD HOTEL STAFF ARE DISPENSING GAS MASKS
NOW BILL ARE YOU STILL THERE BILL? GOT A CALL
FROM UPSTAIRS PAUL CNN DECLARES WAR
HAS STARTED TIME TO GO WE DON'T NEED YOU
THERE ANYMORE.

The War Reporter Paul Watson in the Ali Baba Room

Underneath the One Thousand and One Nights
Disco, where that psycho Uday used to
shake his groove thang. Behind high-pressure steel
blast doors, One Hundred and One Iraqis
in their PJs and bathrobes. An infant
suckling from a bottle while ballistic
concrete winces. Calling to mind graphics
on TV of laser-guided missiles
inserting themselves delicately down
air shafts. A keffiyeh gives me a slug
from his JD's. When lights go out dancing
effervesces in the witching whiteness
of a TV crew's Klieg light. *Palestine
is Arab! Down, Bush, down!* Some Americans
huddled to their smuggled shortwave radio
are cracking up at the newsman's advice
to keep our heads down and our dials tuned
to the BBC. A Canadian
Emmy Award winner had suggested
I drink the beer in his bathtub. Tossed me
pressure bandages for sucking chest wounds
that reporters call maxi pads. Dried prunes.
Half a rattling jar of iodine pills
for roof water. Offered to take me to
Amman tomorrow. *I just got here so
how can I leave? Open, O Sesame!*
sing the sirens. Gazing through double-glazed
windows on a desert city encased
in bomb dust like snow. Ministry buildings
cored to their roots, latticed walls left standing
upright like Western façades. Neighboring

homes stunned yet pristine. The morning commute
coalescing. I take off my clothes and
stretch out on the bed, no longer caring
who's watching from behind the mirror. *This
isn't what I came here for. This won't be
my father's war.*

The War Reporter Paul Watson Regrets the Escape

Riding shotgun in lotus position
like Buddha on my suitcase. The driver
drowns his hands in moonshine. The keychain fob
in the form of the first George Bush's head
swinging like a plumb bob. Somebody's carved
DOWN in his forehead. Mr Ramadan
weaving the wreck-strewn autobahns beneath
crisscrossing contrails of Shiva's warplanes
escorting Tomahawks, while the Beatles
sing "Help!" on the tape deck. Christlike soldiers
wave us through the gates. Morning in Jordan
at the barred Window of Shame, journalists
mingling in a scrum for visas. Black nights
in the jazz bar hounding Mr Adnan,
the visa-man pinching women's buttocks
while addicts beg him to help us return
to death. Shivering beside a mountain
of sodden suitcases in a sudden
downpour along the border, recording
this war I'm missing. *I was sleeping and
I woke up to my blanket burning and
when I reached out to find my son I found
flesh* – and when this weeping father buries
his face in the mud at my feet, I swear
to never let this happen again.

The Poet Asks the Graduate Student

And diabetes. Each summer the ice melts
and the chemicals end up in the food
-chain: kelp, krill, fish, seals, bears, muskox, men. Breast
-feeding's discouraged. And without hunting
the men end up discouraged and then kill
themselves. And of course there's the drinking. Tons
of unwed teenage moms. Teenagers think
of jail like summer camp. Assault, rape. Drugs
would be a problem if there was a way
to get the drugs up here. You should see them
in their black robes and white faces. Families
watching their kids get sentenced on the ice
rink at school, and everybody's crying
and crying. It's colonial. We should try
to keep our voices down. Let me close this
door. There. Here's what I know: an old woman
said how this one time when she was a girl
she hopped off her sled and another sled
just ran her down. And this shaman, I wish
I could remember his name! he climbs out
of his sled and whispers, *Shh*. He removes
all her clothing. He lays her out naked
on the ice, and he rubs her bruised body
everywhere. This old woman remembers
waking up the next morning a healthy
girl again. So why do you care so much
about shamans, Dan? Do you know someone
who needs to get healed?

The War Reporter Paul Watson's Looking for His Story

I can't decide what to write about: art
or these God damned Olympics. Or crime. Cause
there's something shady going on here with
the white guys who run this place. Kickbacks or
maybe something worse? Maybe it's better
not to stir things up too much? don't want to
end up in a snowdrift, right? Popping pills
from his daily-chambered plastic pill case
for depression, high blood pressure, poly
-cystic kidney disease, which reminds me
to take my Zoloft. Which reminds Paul of
the postprandial palaver from racist
construction crews. *Cold and snow, I'll show you
cold and snow! If the seal's still squirming, slit
the little bastard's throat. Eat the raw red
liver, hop on the snowmobile back to
the prefab house, get drunk on lamp fuel and
pass out while your ADHD kids burn
in the fire of said house.* Once some racist
construction workers were fucking someone
on the other side of the wall. Outside
I saw her stepping through the snow, fourteen
at most. Pink parka swollen and shouldering
her schoolbag. Outraged I called the Mounties
and they answered, Who gives a damn? They don't
have a word for consent. It's offensive
to the likes of you and me. But this town's
not like that, Dan. It's peaceful. As far as
anyone can tell.

The War Reporter Paul Watson and the Prostitutes

Children playing war while their mothers tend
to business upstairs. Men nursing bottles
of rice beer waiting for their turn, tossing
cards on curbstones. Herbalists hock sharks' teeth
for bed-wetting, atomized sawfish snout
for pain-killing, snips of twisted branches
for hernias. Climbing a spiral staircase
tasting ammonia, startling rats. Yoga
will strengthen your yoni, she says. Young men
are best seduced from behind. Mattresses
must be knee-high, walls salmon pink. Red paste
called alta smeared along the bloodless soles
of a young girl's feet will inspire a man
with his encroaching death. Bodyworkers
in East Java are forced to thread padlocks
through zippers. *It's difficult to say no
to men. They persuade with their dangerously
sweet words.* At the end of an alleyway
a clot of red balloons towed by a man
buffets past a tower of rotting trash
to climb the protesting fire escape up
to Congress House. Where women sit barefoot
on onyx marble in batik kaftans
mesmerized by their TV soap. Citrus
scent of freshly shampooed hair is wafting
beneath the ticking ceiling fan. Cell phones
blinking on a shelf. Ever since the ban
on gentlemen's clubs they have no choice but
to cake rouge on their faces like schoolgirls
sleeping over, changing into saris
of venereal rose, before heading out

to fuck the men they once danced for. Don't tell
a soul, Dan, but one night I paid a girl
in the dim limbo of Sanam Luang
to tell me her age, and when she took me
by the hand into the open sewer
of a tamarind tree and her voice was
a blade, I felt a shame I still can not
name.

The War Reporter Paul Watson Goes to Hollywood

to try selling my memories. Glass fountains
in the atrium ejaculating
story after story. His luminous
secretary whispered he's so sorry,
It's the freeways. Would you like a bottle
of sparkling water? When the agent came
he confided, I fucked her. You should've
heard her scream!

The War Reporter Paul Watson's Cold Open

A reporter and a photographer
in the age-old Explorer. Exterior
slash interior. Hand-held cam. American
journalists, one should note. Save for this French
fotog up front. With their Afghan driver
sweating. What's-his-name. Being a veteran
war junkie, and French, the Frenchman's frowning
on artists making art en route and thus
keeps his window tight. His process is to
get inside the face of agony, hopefully
as strafing unzips the background. Close up
on our sexy photographer snapping
pics through her open window, sweeping locks
of honeyed hair behind a lamb's ear while
the reporter beside her is voiding
all hunger from his eyes. The incipient
lovers rib our Frenchman. *Safari rules
not good enough for you?* The driver crawls
past a tragic bazaar. Lots of money
-shots for retinal displays. Our American
lowers her viewfinder on a burqa
-smothered mother hurrying with a mewling
newborn. The newborn's almost unborn while
this mother's like a smudge, a blur. A hand
grenade squirts the open window, glancing
off the telephoto, ricocheting
off the Frenchman's closed window and settling
between his feet. Fumbling the door open
wide he's scissoring his boots like a danseur
in a sidelong entrechat, till the blast
severs both legs at mid-thigh. The ringing

in our audience's ears does not stop
the Americans from clasping the Frenchman
while he bleeds out. Their Afghan driver flicks
his tongue like he's tasting a face leathern
with burns. His arm's an unearthed bone. They flag
down a passing Humvee. The cherubic
commander protests he's not allowed to
bring Afghans home. So our heroes leave him
smoldering in the smoldering cab as shadows
approach like men. Fade out, fade in. That night
the reporter and the photographer
fuck like rabbits. Stoned on hash, drunk on death
choosing them. Opening credits and our first
commercial break.

The War Reporter Paul Watson Remembers a Flight

from somewhere blood-lacquered. She was stalking
next to me. A journalist too. She asked,
Do you want to fuck in the bathroom? Not
in so many words. Gunshot eyes ranging
and scored. Her voice as trenched and denuded
as my own. Otherwise delicately
caressing my upper thigh. Who knows why
I suspected she was already dead
when she spilt her cup of tea purposely
in my crotch. Then innocently slipped off
with some other slob. All of us listening
to the beating sobs of their lovemaking
at 30,000 feet flying away
from another man-made tragedy.

The War Reporter Paul Watson on the Bombing of the Dead

A snow-silenced cemetery adjacent
to the fuel depot. A bomb blast blots out
the memory field. Resurrected hands
clatter against windowpanes. The unhinged
skull in a sleeping garden. Bold femurs
stand up in viscous mud. Coffins rising
like broken rafts on a frozen wake. Whorls
of air bore through names and dates. Remorseful
statuary angels wade into bone
chips like a stone strand. A specter in black
sits rocking and waiting for the roaring
jets to pass, a naked cadaver sprawled
at her feet. *My son,* she wails. *Why would they
do this to me? You can not kill the dead
twice.*

The War Reporter Paul Watson and the Professors

Learned men lead us blindly down the stairs
to the women's bathroom in the basement
of the Economics building. Wallets
in the sink, spigots dripping. The bodies
of a professor, a cook and a guard
in orbits of cooling blood. A hammer
beside the professor's glasses, lenses
face-down in his famous brains. Thinnish wrists
bound as if praying with leather laces
from his yawning shoes, black duct tape wound round
hair, nose, cheeks, eyes, mouth. The cook reclines wedged
on her toilet seat. Bindi-like bullet
wound a drooling shock. The swollen tongue stuffed
in the guard's mouth is his clip-on tie. Serbs
or Albanians? inquires the British
soldier with his head in the door. Serbians,
says a voice from the hallway. No problem,
says the Brit. A professor steps into
the light as if to educate us: No
– problem.

The War Reporter Paul Watson Waits in Line

Drunk border guards take my cell phone. Batteries
from my radio. Ray-Bans, rolls of Kodak
film and both Leathermen. So I get by
on past-due yogurt, pickles and garlic
sausage. When I can keep it down. Showering
in Poland Springs. Deciphering my scribbled
notes in the TV's sick flicker. Quarantined
in the not-at-all-Grand Hotel listening
for the whistling incoming. My window
keeps tabs on my rental car. Serbians stab
Leathermen in locks, replacing slashed tires
like kids rolling hoops. And all I can do
is take their picture. Columns of ethnic
Albanians in motleyed parkas driven
like Jews out of a wormhole to the trains
to Macedonia. And all I can do
is wait in line at dawn with the twisted
elderly. Women and priests. They will see
my missing hand and imagine I'm touched
by war. Warm parcels of bread if only
I can learn to hold my tongue. *But tell me*
where are your darlings? Toppled in a stream
like a tangled trunk. Holes in their heads drain
brains into the rapids singing. Screaming
teens are liberating laptops. Satanic
smoke through gap-toothed windows. Raped metal grilles
bent back by crowbars. My spiral notepad's
soaking up sweat in my groin. I give them
the Albanian for reporter. *Tell me*
where you come from? he asks in English. Shit
-eating grin replies, Hotel. Canada

because nobody's ever accused us
of anything. *Why are you here?* Walking.
Watching. That's all. *Then I will watch you walk*
back to the hotel and I will kill you
tonight. God's great aim. God's executioner
draining my poisoned skull. Walking away
to wait in line with the living to fill
this empty bag.

The War Reporter Paul Watson at the Widow's House

Sunny Hill, Pristina. At a schoolhouse
where yesterday a boy got shot running
away. His body rots on his heels. Keep
back from the windows, this mother orders
her children, who are coughing and smearing
noses along their coat sleeves. A neighbor
pressed his pistol into her daughter's rose
-bud cheek, Where is Baba? Before burning
their house to cinders. The classroom concrete
leaches the heat from your bones. So they lay
their heads on desks and slip out of focus
like psychopaths and slaves. *Can we help them
escape?* Either way it will be a sin,
you know. Stepping outside their mother shouts,
Do not make a sound! My translator is
asking zombies at cratered crossroads, Where
are the checkpoints now? Policemen's faces
absolved in balaclavas are seeking
justice. U-turns and dust plumes down side roads
till we find the widow's house. Who stands black
beneath her lintel. A shawl like a caul
across her sunken mouth. I can't even
help myself! she cries, peering through pissing
sleet at my idling Opel. I withdraw
some filthy bills. Driving away glimpsing
the youngest son's open palm slapping on
the window of the widow's house. *U-turns
and dust plumes down side roads.*

In the parking lot of the hospital
nurses are lifting their heads in pursuit
of surface-to-air missiles swiveling
up through the trees like spermatozoa
spraying gold ash, outraced by the barrel
-rolling bomber larking higher. *Come on
baby, hit something this time.* Cluster bombs
have scattered the spines and axles of carts
in the road. A young mother's spread-eagled
on hard-baked mud ruts, frantically sucking
in her final breaths. A tidal carpet
-blast danced this mother's mother over wire
and wed her to a tree. A tow-haired doll
reposes in a burning bush. Whimpering
of a grandchild somewhere. The scratching chick
inside its stone egg. Alcoa-stamped fin
fragments in the rubble. The fog of war
as crematorium smoke. Infiltrating
ruins for rifles, uniforms, a shred
of evidence. So many refugee
corpses on folding tables. A child's face
in his terrycloth sleeper is peppered
with shrapnel like freckles. Hematomaed
eyes like Mama's eye shadow. Watery
blood like juice or afterbirth. Head lifted
into the fluorescent lights. Mouth open
against the plastic pane. Teeth and tongue poised
for speaking as for crying. Blurred as if
breathing, as if only sleeping until
this war is over.

The War Reporter Paul Watson Remembers the War Reporter Jana Schneider

Jana and Slovenian reporter
Ivo Standeker were crossing a field
of mud, when an explosion sent Jana
fifteen yards through the air before hitting
the ground on the back of her head. Shrapnel
burning in her thighs. Yelling to Ivo
to leave her. After a mortar bomb ripped
out his spine, she had a heart attack. Once
she had a recording contract. Wowing
audiences on Broadway as Helena
Landless in *The Mystery of Edwin Drood*,
snarling like a tigress and slithering
her s's, her nails like eagles' talons
shredding air, said the *Times*. She almost won
a Tony Award. Then at 35
decided there wouldn't be any more
roles for her. And so borrowed a camera
and went to Sri Lanka. Then Angola,
Pakistan, India, Cuba, Baghdad,
Sarajevo. Photos on the covers
of *Time* and *Newsweek*. She'd easily tell
you how she'd been kidnapped, raped and tortured
more than once. She had this way of speaking
that sounded like a lie. Then one morning
she stood at my door asking to borrow
a blanket. She was sleeping in her car
in a game preserve outside Johannesburg
while starring in a TV commercial
for Volvo that would require her to chase
a Dakota plane in the candescent
African dawn. Then a few days later

my blanket immaculately folded
appeared on my doorstep. Ten years later
she ranted on the steps of a brownstone
in the Village, plastic bags around her
feet full of clothes, cardboard, a zipper bag
of panhandled change, scraps of donated
pizza. A black leather outback duster
over a sweater, sweatpants, two ski hats.
Police charged her with boisterousness. Bellevue
diagnosed her with psychosis brought on
by schizophrenia, then locked her away
with other madwomen. Who slept on air
mattresses on particle boards. Doctors
made her attend classes on how to read
newspapers. *What is this photograph of,
Miss Schneider? Do you know?* At the hearing
she stood up and said, My name *is* Jana
Schneider. And it *is* true that I received
a Tony nomination. And it's also
true I was a famous photojournalist
in numerous war zones. She was remanded
into the care of her mother, returned
to the desolate fields of McFarland,
Wisconsin, where I went to visit her
not too long ago, and when she opened
her arms to me I wish I had taken
her picture.

The War Reporter Paul Watson on the Knock at the Door

Lying in bed with the lights off listening
to bombs detonating like a storm rolling
away over a summer lake. The knock
at my door's desperate, lovesick. Hammering
like the Grand Hotel Pristina might split
apart like socialism. Herding crews
into the hallway like Goya's *May 3rd,*
1808. Lining up some weeping
newsmen for execution, opening fire
into the drywall beside their heads. *Slide*
into the coffin beneath your bed. Fear
is what they're after. Why are you tempted
to give him what he wants? The rifle butt's
slapping the lock in my socket. A gruff
word calls him off. My disappointed love
sighs, berating himself. Mud-smothered soles
on mildewed carpeting. When the battering
picks up at my neighbor's door someone's voice
cries out and they kick her door in. A rule
that's always served me well: When your knock comes,
don't answer.

The War Reporter Paul Watson Listens to Isaac

In Kumasi you come out of the womb
playing soccer, mon. In the street barefoot
with a bunch of trash bags taped together
or a rotten orange and you kick that
from gutter to gutter. My father was
an engineer who drives a taxi now
in Yellowknife. Ha ha ha. Armed Forces
Revolutionary Council Supreme
Military Council Provisional
National Defence Council National
Liberation National Redemption
Councils – I can't keep all these councils straight
in my head, mon! Ha ha ha. My mom was
a speechwriter. A soldier in the street
tore her shirt off and made her suck the tip
of his AK-47 before
he pulled the trigger. Yeah, so. Now I work
for the Canadian government. Flying
across the Arctic teaching the People
of the North how to play soccer. I give
them jerseys, hoodies, water bottles and
new soccer balls. I'm usually the first
black face they've ever seen! I like to say,
Where I was born isn't that different from
where you are now. In terms of not being
noticed. But all they can ask me is how
do I stand the cold?

The War Reporter Paul Watson in the Colonies

The dictator favored Savile Row suits
and homburg hats. Fondled his lion's tail
whisk for flies. Bussed in whores to welcome him
with ululations as he descended
Airstairs to the tarmac. Boys with long hair,
girls in trousers and kissing in public
were jailable offenses. Providence
Secondary School's Sister Mary Joy
Magombo shelved her wimple. A heart-sick
West Yorkshire widow drunk at noon pursued
students with her bush knife. My manor stood
in the mahogany shade, tribes of vervets
launching sorties on Biblical fig trees
inflecting my dreams. Mulanje Massif
like Atlantis rising from an ocean
of susurrous green tea terraces. *This thin
white line.* Past which my barefoot cook called me
"Bwana." Mr Banda the cadaver
-faced commerce teacher with a bookworm wife
and an inveigling eye. Chakwanira
taught biology with snuff suspended
in his young beard like Darwin. Named his child
after the first one died "We Who Are Still
Mourning." As soon as the bells tolled we'd sit
like those proverbial monkeys, sipping piss
-warm Carlsberg Greens. *There are witch doctors known
for their love potions. Better than hashish
bundled in banana leaves, tied tight with
butcher's twine and compacted over time
into nubs like coal cobs that will explode
your mind!* Mr Banda at Bwana's door

with sisters in scandalous décolletage, thongs
splitting burnished toes. Giggling observing
their professors blaze up. Mr Banda
locked my bedroom door, my girl took my hand
and babbled me down to the floor. Reeling
from the punch of the hash and her sweat. *Go
now! Get out – everyone!* Banda emerged
with brown penis flapping. Sisters weeping
so sweetly. *You should give them soap at least
for their time.*

The War Reporter Paul Watson and the Secret of War

Das Afrikaner spelled my name in blood
-red Sharpie on cardboard. Woolen knee socks
and safari boots whisking me away
to his tarnished silver Dakota plane
like *Casablanca*. One seat packed inside
a columbarium of gun crates, courtesy
of US taxpayers. A sandwich wrapped
in plastic, a six-pack sloshing the ice
in the Igloo. Hot, buzzing, the strumming
turbines lulled me to sleep, the cockpit lights
woke me up. Through the window the oil lamps
lined the secret airstrip like a churning
Amazonian dead end. Minstrelsy eye
-balls peering out of the jungle beneath
a sword of Damocles moon. I thought, *This
will be a very cool war.* Liaisoning
with Dr Jonas Savimbi bunkered
beneath a camp of wicker huts, listening
to Bach on his 8-track. A preacher's son
in the snug red beret. A heavyweight
boxer's bovine arms. Cinematic smile
and a syphilitic mind. You and I
are the same, he told me. Everyone wants
to drink and to laugh! Although friends became
witches to be burned alive. Harrowing
his own countryside with landmines like trees
of death that spring up with branches fruiting
feet and hands and heads. At a hospital
treating limbless Angolans, Angolan
-born son of Portuguese settlers Dr
Chassanha asked me if I'd lost my hand

in battle. No, I said, it was an act
of God. I have been wounded several times,
he explained, one shot severed every nerve
on this side here. But here is the secret
of war: the more wounds the better. The chaste
swoon at their first caress. On a winding
deserted road in Kandahar I pray
one doctor was right and the other was
wrong.

The War Reporter Paul Watson and the Mountain Gorillas

Knuckle-walking the slope of a sleeping
volcano, squeezing nettles like razors
to keep from sliding back. Sunrise weaving
light into a canopy of hanging
moss like lynchings. Rows of sapling crosses
stuck in the mud, nailed with aluminum
nameplates. *The old lady in the forest
without a man.* Boxing Day and poachers
husked her ruddy crown. Digit the sentry
silverback held the men at bay until
his mate could escape. Beating their leaping
basenji into the earth as lances
sliced his side like Golgotha. Head hacked off
for a trophy, hands on sale as ashtrays
for 10 dollars US. A dozen beasts
and Fossey in their graves. *In the Clearing*
on her shelf. *Nature within her inmost
self divides / To trouble men with having
to take sides.* A family of gorillas
lounging and swatting, cracking and munching
stems and roots and bamboo shoots. Drowsily
nit-picking in the tweed of their nests. Chimps
will seize you by the throat and suck the blood
from your caverned nose, drag your shattered leg
downslope to Burenge where yesterday
a famished boy gazed into my camera
while giving up the ghost. While the hooting
silverback closes his eyes like a girl
climaxing, demurely. Grunting, growling
like a ventriloquist with a cold. Pounding
leathered pectorals with cupped palms so pockets

of alarm echo. Then and only then
does he unhinge his human fangs. *Nature*
troubling men to take sides. Diane Fossey's
corpse beside her gun, almost loaded. When
the upstart male relents, a ball of fluff
with a mesa of afro and black eyes
like the daughter I don't have, knuckle-walks
over to my horripilating legs, sniffs
my cursed camera before somersaulting
into the forest.

The War Reporter Paul Watson Considers the Peacekeepers

At the traffic circle I see hundreds
of men, women and children, some waving
branches. The blue and white flag. Reciting
Aideed's name. Pakistani peacekeepers
open fire so I hug the wall. Trying
to meld with the brick. A drill hammer. Pause
and somebody's moaning. Bursts of gunfire
and a child screaming. A man is pleading,
Stop! Please stop! A crack. Then another. Then
nothing. Nothing moves. I turn to the sound
of moaning. He's maybe seven, lying
on his side in the street. While I'm standing
in a web of rippled gray mush. No blood
on him. The top of his head's sliced open
like an eggshell. The skull's completely white
and empty as if someone's wiped it clean
with a cloth. A spray from a machine gun
blew his brains out. That's what I've been standing
in. With his father lying beside him
facedown, an arm behind his back. He's cut
almost in half. Bullets perforated
his belly. The moaning is a woman
next to them, rocking back and forth, *Allah*,
Allah. Peacekeepers in their armored trucks
looking down on us as they drive around
and out of the circle.

The War Reporter Paul Watson Listens to Mohammed

Because simply I was shown a picture
in school. Teacher explaining, These houses
are made of ice! While outside the burning
undercarriage of a car, white children
as coal. Their mother sleeping in the road
with her skirt above her face. Husband's hands
melting to the wheel, a fiery halo
of hair like Jesus Christ. The faceless face
of la guerre sans nom. Polypropylene
pipes have burst and my own shit and piss stains
the ice of an Arctic dawn. I'm sorry
my house smells like the slowest backwaters
of the Casbah, but I have always known
I would be blessed to die here, if only
I could make it.

The War Reporter Paul Watson and Dirty Business

On foot, Somalia and Afghanistan
are the same. Combat boots sink ankle-deep
in the bone-gray talc, bursts of jetting earth
coating teeth and lenses. The peacekeepers
in Belet Huen baited petty thieves with
food and water. Shot a man in the back
as he ran. Could not lift his black body
without it flopping to pieces. A boy
found hiding in a toilet. Some soldiers
waterboarded him, then sodomized him
with a broomstick. Extinguished cigarettes
on his penis. Then beat him with meal packs
till he died. At a miserable crossroads
years later, things are done neatly. When roads
leap out in shrapnel and claim another
soldier for death, a bulldozer disrobes
the walls of a Pashtun village. Money
changes hands, teenagers handed over
to police for torture. Even children
race from the peacekeepers as they approach
on foot. White faces under blue helmets
tell me: It's dirty business, but then war
always is.

The War Reporter Paul Watson Chases the Lion of Panjshir

His house was as he left it. Hand grenades
from China, Russian land mines and rocket
-launchers, boxes of steel-enveloped slugs
from Iran. Piled neck-high in the backyard
next to a milking machine. Satellite dish
on the roof, riding lawnmower sinking
in the weeds. Treadmill inside for battling
insurgent love handles. His library
was rumored to house over a thousand
classics of world literature. While Talibs
who know only the Koran were oiling
their Kalashnikovs on the veranda,
I was leafing through a biography
of Thomas Jefferson. Where is Massoud
now? Warrior-poet, his dusty pakul
hat canted like a beret. Reciting
Persian poetry as accurately as
mortar range. So I hired an '82
Soviet Lada, seats upholstered in sin
-ful velveteen, black iron bars spanning
door to door to keep its rusted body
from shuddering to pieces. A dashboard sleek
with silver fox fur, a silver serpent
twisting from the rearview mirror because
whenever a snake appears in your dreams
money will come slithering your way. I paid
him 50 dollars. The Hindu Kush rose
like the opaque veil of death. Shell craters
and potholes like ponds made our Lada buck
and spasm in the slush, behind a bus
of Sony Trinitron TVs that spun

from a treacherous turn, toppling and crushing
a shepherd boy. My driver went looking
for his shoes in the mud. Starving we stopped
at a kebab house full of Taliban
oiling their Kalashnikovs with ardor
as usual. The Muslim sabbath. Ogling
girls in cherry swimsuits gamboling across
the beach on *Baywatch*. Waking to Lada
stuck in the ice like Snow White in her glass
coffin, we ladled out a precious sheen
of gasoline to light a fire to melt us
free. Years later I'm waiting in Moscow
for my visa while Massoud and a friend
lie on mattresses on the floor. Riffling
pages of the Sufi poet Hafiz,
whose ghazals picked at random can foretell
the future. Massoud's friend lays his finger
on this verse: *O you who have been waiting*
together, value this night. All nights turn
into morning. When some Arab journalists
arrive unannounced. Is he a wrestler
or a photographer? Who are you? We
are Muslim. Why do you hate bin Laden?
Why do you call him a murderer? Switch
on your camera, says Massoud. Explosions
make night of this world. The assassins' flesh
becomes piercing rain. Massoud's friend cries, God
save us! A hand on my wrist: the last touch
of Massoud, says the friend. Gone with the breath
of our prayers.

The War Reporter Paul Watson and the Boys with the Bomblet

A gang of shepherd boys minding their own
rib-caged cows. When a yellow can appears
in a dust cloud. Like soda or a sleeve
of tennis balls, clasped in a corona
of tabs known as The Spider. Casing scored
so as to better shatter in a blast
of stampeding shrapnel that will strip all
clothes and flay any naked skin, leaving
pulped, cauterized stumps. Tinkling like wind chimes
after the wetter thuds. *The tiny chute
hangs limply from the lip.* Designed to drift
silently, otherworldly, increasing
our scatter radius. Preset to detonate
at precise heights or times. Or with the thrum
of traffic, the plosives of speech. Tremors
of the lightest footfalls. Two boys running
off in search of a father. The one boy
holding the canister suggests, Maybe
we'll find some food inside? The other one
slips his knife beneath the tab to find out
what's inside The Spider.

The War Reporter Paul Watson and the Economy of War

Scrap merchants are decapitated so
scavengers root through the graveyards and dumps
for human bones to bundle up in cords
at eight cents a kilo. Then the dealers
export their cargo at 20 percent
profit to Pakistan, where the bone meal
of Afghans becomes the ingredients
in hand soap and surprisingly potent
fertilizer. The vineyards and orchards
of Afghanistan wilt. Poppies blooming
red in the wind on their delicate green
stems.

Like a movie killer the drugs hunter
keeps snapshots like trophies. As if playing
a losing hand of cards. Pakul, kufi
skullcap. Crooked Afghan policemen cuffed
beside their grenades and guns. A half ton
of opium in a tanker, musk masked by
the sweet rot of canary melons. Not
a man in jail. Kunduz is half an hour
from Tajikistan, 24 hours from
Moscow, Milan, London. Pluffing pompoms
and brass bells jingling on ponies pulling
carts through dusk. The sergeant with iconic
eyes like Alexander wheezes closing
his basement window. The informant says,
Most families have a dozen barrels and
a pressing machine, cotton filters and
acetic anhydride for refining
paste to powder. Enough poppies have been
stashed in wells and rusted tanks to outlast
a lifetime of crackdowns. In the lobby
of the station Ziploc bags smeared with tar
-like opium gum. Hash blocks. Pouring the pure
heroin across tiles, granules finer
than sand. Like trying to clear the sand from
the desert, and we all laugh. Our government
is no government, they say. We hope and pray
for that day when our invader becomes
our boss. Bulgarian rose seedlings poke through
sulfurous soil that used to yield gladsome fields
of flashing blood and cash. Now when the wind
bruises new roses they're rendered worthless

to French perfumiers. Farmers have only
a day to decapitate and express
their romantic oils. If this idea works,
one farmer tells me, then Afghanistan
will be famous for flowers like Paris
is famous for whores! His face a skull from
years of smoking the fecal, floral ball
grins in the sun. The smuggler in his cell
shrugs his shoulders at me. The more smugglers
in jail, the more others will make profit.
The professional businessmen will remain
because of connections. Whoever works
hardest in business will always endure.

The War Reporter Paul Watson Remembers the Freedom Fighter Abdul Haq

Peshawar. He hugged me at the front door,
limping on his prosthesis. We were both
missing things, though a landmine took his foot
while I was born this way. He was wearing
a white shalwar kameez. Like Rob Reiner
with a tan. Fifteen years before he'd been
the bane of the Soviets. His guerillas
cascading down mountain slopes as nimbly
as mountain goats. Wearing the pakul hat
on the sea foam couch across from Ronald
Reagan. Beneath the ivy-topped mantel
in the Oval Office. The Taliban
and the ISI broke in his front door
and murdered his young wife and youngest son
not long ago. I begged him, *Let me go
with you!* But he just smiled and my fixer
translated, No. Waking up on the floor
outside Kabul. Dried blood like Rorschach blots,
shells underfoot, holes in the clay. Bathing
from a communal bucket, one toilet
overflowing with shit. Everybody
had dysentery. And some asshole asked me,
Have you heard what happened to Abdul Haq?
He came over the Khyber Pass last week
with two dozen men and the Taliban
ambushed him. Down in the crenellated
canyon all night on his satellite phone
begging the CIA to send a drone
but no one came for him. In the morning
they captured him and cut off his dick and
stuffed it in his mouth. Hanged him from a tree

with a metal noose. Shot up his body
till he just swung there like meat. I'm sorry,
Dan. I'm so sorry! I have no idea
why I'm thinking about him. I don't know
why I'm crying either, it wasn't me
who ignored his calls. I wasn't the one
who killed him. I'm not even American
like you!

The War Reporter Paul Watson Listens to the Teacher

The upstairs room was vacant, corpse-like men
in plastic shoes hawked the clothes of corpses
down at roadside. A tailor worked a foot
-pumped sewing machine in the shop below
my feet. Somewhere somebody was fashioning
steel into replacement doors. The windows
shuddered with each pang of their exhausted
hammering. Welders' hacksaws and torches
blowing and gnawing through scraps. When the fall
forgave the Hindu Kush with snow and wind
skinned the city, I wore a woolen shawl
over my winter coat. Electric lights
stayed off for safety. I searched the bazaars
for old chairs with broken seats. My blackboard
was plywood brushed with black paint. I dissolved
chalk in water and painted the mud walls
white. That afternoon, the sun was setting
and every girl's seat was empty. The boys
sat with their copies of the *Kabul Times*
opened like Korans in their laps. Outside
Russian Volgas, Toyota Landcruisers
with their windows tinted black, donkey carts
choking the exodus. Horns celebrating
every escaped soul. *Tomorrow morning*
we'll have class as usual. But if we don't
see each other again, this is goodbye
forever. Slipping the barnacled lock
through the rings in the door, I rode my bike
home in darkness. Pedaling, the gathering
of my death on the horizon. I climbed
to the roof of our house. The road soaring

with tanks, truck-borne rocket launchers, anti
-aircraft guns. The panicked columns winding
towards the city's northern gates. Headlights
mystifying the dust. I sat and watched
another army advancing after
another army's left. And then climbed down
and went to work, hoping I'd find some peace
in tomorrow's lesson.

The War Reporter Paul Watson and Ghosts of the Hindu Kush

Every stone in the Khaibar's been baptized
in blood. Said the Brit famously. Soldiers
in our watchtowers hear spirits cursing
in Russian behind them. Pakistani
smugglers whisper tales of orbs like the wraiths
of raped girls. With albino-pink eyes and
Caucasoid skin. Blood-slaked tongues. I refused
to wear the burqa and so had to feign
sleep in the backseat. Jubilant Pashtuns
mimed, Roll down your window! At a mudbrick
compound like a Saturday matinee
of *Gunga Din*, a fistful of twenties
slipped our chains. A highway of depressions
sewn with shrapnel. Osama bin Laden's
stronghold nearby. Found my guide, my teacher
in a broken chair in a cold classroom
in Kabul. Watching the windowsill weep
icicles. A woolen shawl securing
his buttonless duffle coat. Ink-black beard
two hands long. No friend of the Taliban,
he assured me. I asked, Will you lead me
north? He smiled. After midnight unscrewing
the hissing radiator cap. Pissing
into a Pepsi can. Piddling, praying
for far more substantial streams. The rumor
of deliquesced glaciers out there beyond
a moonless minefield. My Maglite a torch
-led procession of monks stepping lightly
in the catacombs. Even Macedon
skulls underfoot. When my guide, my teacher
shouts, Stop! – the cliff's edge, the river giggling

like children scattering. Every innkeeper
was sleeping, so the watchman with his lamp
banged on metal doors for us. When we woke
in the bedchamber of our car, bullhorns
girding minarets, muezzins droning
Allahu Akbar! shaking mulberries
out of the dawn, the dead were sleeping while
the snow pigeons bounced. My guide, my teacher
ignores my calls and emails now. I hope
he's still no friend of the Taliban but
this war has gone on so long I suspect
he's no longer a friend of mine.

The War Reporter Paul Watson on the Examination of Women

Clean-shaven men are criminals. Cassettes
get unspooled and strung from checkpoint towers
festively like intestines. All their shoes
are black. Waving hello's taboo. Women
doctors disappear, the female sick must
of course remain at all times enshrouded
in their burqas. As the doctor reaches
under the hem to feel only the part
of her that hurts. To look into her eyes
or at the surface of her tongue would prove
too difficult through the grille. Naturally
female doctors are called back. Male doctors
guide every examination blindly
from behind a closed door, where many hear
sick women bleeding to death. A poet
-doctor named Abdul Hamed once revealed
to me: The Taliban is a mystery
its Creator is unable to solve.

The War Reporter Paul Watson Skypes From Kandahar

Tell them that after I wrote a story
about you, your father the policeman
watched a hand grenade rattling into
white deaf night. Tell them you claimed his body
off the mosque floor. Tell them you heard a voice
snarling across the phone line accusing
you of defiling young girls by teaching
them the Internet. Tell them they've promised
to rape then murder your older sisters
in front of you. But you mustn't forget
what your father used to teach you: Either
your country or a coffin. *Let me say
how compelling we all find your story,
Roya. Our graduates include the actor
Matthew Perry. Of* Friends. *But we're concerned:
can you pass our entrance exam?* She will
become a politician. She will return
to Kandahar one day. *Thank you, Mr
Watson. But we'd like to hear this girl speak
for herself.* This girl who can't stop sobbing
for all that she's learned. *Either your country
or a coffin.*

The War Reporter Paul Watson Listens to Roya Shams, 17, Describe Her Gift

I call his cell phone and tell him, Come home
for breakfast. But then the shooting started
and he died. My father was responsible
for Sub-station # 1, he got shot
a few times in the past. He was working
for security forces since he was
the age I am now, in every government
and regime. Never had we tried to flee
to Iran. We felt, We are not living
in Kandahar! because of the freedom
he gave us. I have five older sisters
and one is a doctor. One brother is
a doctor also. Insurgents pretend
illness, so Mother tells them, The doctors
are not home. We find night letters hanging
on our door, promising to never tire
of targeting us, even to target
our babies in the cradle. If we seek
refuge in any part of the country
they will find us. The lion my father
is finished, and my family are jackals,
they tell us. When the old man was living
we made many suicide attempts and now
we are making plans to use a car bomb
to kill you all, they tell us. If a chance
is given, I must find a way to leave
the country. My father was a hero
to us all but – words are making me fail
to tell of him! sometimes I can not hold
myself and see: tears do fall. I agree
that many love my mother more but he

was most beloved by me. BBC News
was what he called me. Because we discussed
many issues. You will become famous
one day, like the BBC. But country
or coffin. You must choose. Definitely
I am proud for his martyrdom, I feel
shy speaking of him. But I understand
with one man's permanent absence the world
does not change. At the Kandahar airport
a policeman says, You will not come back.
I promise, If you are still working here
years from now, you will see me walk past you
again. God bless my father and this gift
of mine.

The War Reporter Paul Watson and the Lady Pol

Better they should cover my mouth. They fear
the weal of her voice. Tangerine handbills
like Bollywood. Because she used to read
news on the radio, and then TV,
they accused her of seducing women
to Christ. Kidnapped her husband and crushed his
testicles. She had to lift her burqa
to clamber over walls. Two men clutching
each other on a motorbike appeared
in her side-view mirror. Dragged her screaming
into the middle of a mountain pass
to shoot her till she stopped. One final shot
docked her ear. Her body like a panniers
bleeding into the heaving accordion
ribs of a mountain ass. One bullet lives
encysted in her hip. Then a car bomb
on her way to campaign. Seven vessels
pouring blood. Sobs. Glass like diamonds showered
into the smoking carpet of leaves shocked
out of the trees. *Searching for my own flesh
in the naked branches. When I explain
my reason, no one understands!* Their texts
promise to splash acid in the faces
of my uncovered daughters. I forgive
the Muslims who don't know better. The men
in the street selling shoes – at least their lives
will be improved. My life's already been
spoken for.

The War Reporter Paul Watson and the Chief's Embrace

One in the afternoon, Pashtun police
are fondling bodies at the gate. Chieftains
with uprooted beards, turbans like nests, dust
on the tongues of their sneakers. Gossiping
on conference room couches, slurping mint tea,
collecting cell messages while casting
aspersive glances. The police chief laughs
as he embraces. Slings tobacco juice
towards his spittoon. Another hero
of the Soviet war. With cars exploding
down the road, the road itself exploding
en route to the airfield. Ambulances
exploding the dead. Says the Taliban
is almost finished. *Most murders are due*
to squabbling families. They are all hoping
to join us now. Two in the afternoon
and a man in uniform is waiting
for the chief to step into the courtyard
till they embrace. Cold cylinders pressing
into both their bellies. Wrestling settling
of ball bearings and nails. The man fiddling
with something like a camera trigger till
both men explode. Chunks of corpses rain down
like volcanic cinders. Wind sprints, senseless
shouts. The assassin has taken several
out with the chief, and everyone's wounded
who survives.

The War Reporter Paul Watson Listens to the Translator's Story

Waiting inside, my cell phone chirrups. Joy
is terror. All my unmarried brothers
pass through the gate first. Snaking a taxi
through Kandahar City without any
guards or guns. Wearing a veil so the sun
becomes a maze of heaven. *When you're gone
the rest of us will finally be free
of protecting you!* Laughing and listening
for the sear of the motorbike. Mother
holding me at night. *The walls are hissing,
Escape.* The breathtaking snows of Ottawa,
Vancouver's mourning rain. My wife's feeding
my parents. I say, *If you go with me
I'm happy. If you won't go with me then
this is goodbye.* When they lost their signal
I climbed on top of the wall and lifted
my radio into the air and the bold
splashing molten bronze of bullets until
the calm of their chatter again. Driving
the ambulance all summer. Translating
the dying raging in Pashto, Dari
and English. Standing in blood and feces
like an angel. A sixteen-year-old boy
threw pebbles at a Humvee, one shot punched
through his tattooed chest. Hardly bleeding but
his breathing was like a cistern his eyes
were sinking into. The medic with skin
like the snows of Ottawa was opening
the breast to snake a tube in. I whispered
ceaselessly into the boy's dimming ear
of the lie to come. Till his eyes opened

and I kissed his brow, and the brow went smooth
and the medic stopped. *Snaking a taxi
through Kandahar City without any
guards or guns.* Seeing my face the white clerk
hands me a form letter I must translate
for myself. I'm sorry to inform you
you have not met the criteria. Thank you
for your service to our mission to help
your country one day become a country
that no longer needs our help.

The War Reporter Paul Watson Interviews the Negotiator

Reformer, defector, he'd much rather
stay in bed. Saturnine in his tortoise shell
glasses. Half-empty, smoky. Skeletal
frame wound in a chapan piped with eras
of clay, gold, breath, weeds. Possibly henna
-tinged beard. Nosferatu's ears. Funereal
longi enwreathing his temples. C4
bricks wrapped inside a turban blasted off
his forerunner's face. So our mild mullah
educates Washington. *The Taliban*
will never stop fighting because talking
peace gets us nowhere. You Americans talk
out of both sides of your smiles. Whatever
weapons of mass distraction you possess
your drones have dropped on us. A crone ferrying
chai to us. Liver-spotted hands, deadpan
glance. If it were true I did not support
women, would I have married a doctor
to my only son? The lethargic maid
hangs like a leash. Prunes in the old man's teeth
like oil. Our government has no control
because we must always be answering
to you. And Pakistan. If they want rid
of this violence, we must be taken out
of the equation. The one and only
thing Taliban know for certain is that
they're of the people by the people for
Allah. Stuck in traffic not far from home,
a white Corolla blossoms alongside
the negotiator. Dozing in the rear
of his unarmored Pathfinder without

his bodyguard today. On the way to
this latest colloquy of the Body
for Reconciliation. Wind censing soot
onto his nephew's steering hands. A hand
in the window of the white car simply
aims a pistol that pops like a balloon,
and the nephew doesn't even notice
Rahmani deflating in the rearview
mirror, blood spotting his chapan until
they're streets away and the Corolla has
withered back into the noise. And no one's
claiming credit for his murder, as of
the writing of this poem.

The War Reporter Paul Watson and the Sapper in the Vineyard

Beyond razor wire, sunrise and birdsong
while scrying the road for Styrofoam rocks.
A stovepipe in the mud wall enclosing
a feral vineyard. Venous string wriggling
like a lizard's lost tail. A sledgehammer
bursts forth rusted scraps, barbs of chain link and
shards of butcher's knives. Lug nuts and wrenches
and motorcycle engine blocks. One charge
lifts me up over the road. The next wave
lays me out flat in my grave. Deaf and blind
my hands are dry. Standing. Think about it
and there's nothing to be done! What's the point
of worrying about what you can't control
anymore? Is it going to be this step?
Is it going to be this step? Coming down
confused my hips and spine. Chiropractors
got my vertebrae in line. Suiting up
in combat gear I race a sun setting
beyond razor wire. They're not as strong as
they used to be. We can pretty much go
any day now.

The War Reporter Paul Watson Retells the Story of the Diver and the Goddess

Once there was a beautiful girl. Thank you
for this coffee. Who refused to marry
any Inuk till a stranger comes and
the vacuum cleaner kicks in. Old women
are scrubbing the fryolator. This girl
who by the way is named Sedna I think
gets whisked away to a rocky eyrie
to live with her beloved, who molts his skin
and reveals himself to be naturally
a cormorant. Sedna hates eating fish
every day, like every day these locals
sit here gnawing on their chicken fingers
morosely. So Sedna's father butchers
the birdman for lying. And paddling home
the birdman's bird-friends come and flap the wind
into a gale. The cowardly father
chucks Sedna like Jonah into the sea
where she clings with her fingers to the ledge
of their kayak. So he hacks her fingers
off one by one, and one by one they slip
into the icy, uproarious depths
where her pinky becomes the char, her thumb
the obstreperous walrus, her wedding
finger the narwhal, her middle finger
well you get the point. It's magic. No thanks
I don't want any trinkets. Not now. No
thank you, I said! In the summer cruise ships
come sluicing the lucid Northwest Passage
and dock here. Where was I? Sedna becomes
a vengeful mermaid somehow. With taboos
that say one must give one's seal corpse a sip

of water. For instance. And if hunters
have a dry spell then some shortstraw must swim
to the bottom of the ocean to pick
the tangles from Sedna's hair. The author
of this book lives in Toronto, I need
to interview him about this question
of exploitation. Look at this picture
with hair like threading seaweed and a comb
of scrimshaw. The diver and the goddess
are so entangled they've become transformed
into fucking, mythical characters.

The War Reporter Paul Watson Talks to Himself

If someone says you're worth something you are
immediately suspicious. That person's
an idiot. When they say it's shit you're like,
Hey! I'm not *that* bad. Your mom was always
brainwashing you. *There's nothing the matter*
with your missing hand. All you've got to do
is put yourself out there in the world and
prove it. But everything the world tells you
is opposite. And this is the moment where
we get confused. Everyone's got something
the matter with them, and mine's pretty small,
relatively. So long as I keep my eyes
open. But you don't, do you. It's not death
that frightens you. What is it then? Speaking
of trauma, maybe it's been a kind of
delayed reaction? spending all your life
talking to someone who doesn't want to
talk to you?

The War Reporter Paul Watson Retiring

I'm still hoping to be found by the ghost
of my father. I get that. It doesn't
take much brains. I'm simply willing to go
where no sane person should. And I get praise
for it. Feels good. A colleague once called me,
Adventure Journalist! but the bad guys
who want to kill us aren't hanging out
at the hotel pool. But that's no excuse
for leaving a son without a father
or my wife without income. She begs me
every chance she gets, This is ruining you!
Ha ha ha. She wants to squeeze a promise
out of me. So I say, Okay, you're right,
I'm done. But the moment I get off Skype
I'm planning my next war. I was speaking
to my editor recently and she said,
We're going to have to close down the bureau
soon, at which point I don't know what we'll do
with you. And I was like, Sorry, what's that
supposed to mean? Well, I'm sure you're aware
you have a reputation for being
kind of this quirky reporter. Sucking
dirt in hellholes like Afghanistan and
basically what she's saying is, You're not
useful anymore. Useful was her word
exactly. And it felt like a vacuum
sucking out my guts. And I blew – I blew
my top! First of all. I screamed and I hung
the phone up on her. I have some trouble
waking up still. After lunch I like to
go back to sleep. I'd like to resurrect

myself somehow, I'd love to feel the blood
flooding my veins. But instead the Devil's
got hold of me. Ha ha ha. I suppose
I just have zero tolerance now. The world's
disabused me, so I've simply begun
disabusing myself of the world.

The War Reporter Paul Watson Reviewed

Nobody reads anymore. Do you read
newspapers? Last winter a blizzard raged
like this for fourteen days! That's a fortnight
to Canadians. And nobody's clicking
on my Arctic pieces either. Snow is
whistling under the window and piling
up like mini-shipwrecks. I'd like to skip
these fucking Olympics. Just between you
and me, my confessor. They want me there
when a pipe bomb goes off. I guess I could
become a wedding photographer if
things keep getting worse. Ha ha ha. I could
write movies, or another book. My first
book sold like shit, some critic said: The point
that war's living inside each of us is
neither original nor particularly
helpful. Author Watson's at his best whilst
giving us the sights and sounds of war but
his memoir suffers each time he aspires
to write this kind of poetry whose only
loyalty is to the truth. I'm paraphrasing
now of course. But what kind of prick uses
the word whilst? Author Watson is lifting
his glass to his face, whilst wind swells the room
like a breath before sobbing. Fluorescent
lights and TV stutter. Author O'Brien
screws up his ego. Your book had no point
for me actually. I'd read half a page
then go and wash my hands. Because it was
all too much! I still don't understand how
you keep going. *Have I told you about
the time I met Mother Theresa?*

The War Reporter Paul Watson Meets Mother Theresa

She points towards a chair. *If she's willing*
she will see you. All these shady characters
in Italian business suits. Then after
a week or so another sister stops
halfway down the stairs. *Mother is ready*
now, only for a short while, a moment
if you're lucky. Overhead she's shuffling
around on her crippled kind of bare feet
in this room like a cell with tapestries
respiring in the door frames, back and forth
appearing then swallowed up in the wall
again. Never looking at me because
I'd seen the rows and rows of AIDS victims
and others living on these sorts of cots
very close to the ground. And they don't get
any medical care, they get cleaned up
sometimes, and they get fed. They don't get fed
a lot. So I was trying to be hard
on Mother Theresa, saying, you know,
Don't you think you should be feeding them more
food? Don't you think you should be doing this
or that? And she stops me: They don't need food,
they need love. And she kept on saying that.
They need love. They need love. That's all. That's all.
And I'm thinking, Wow, this is like shooting
ducks in a pond! This woman's a moron,
right? So I go home and I write my hit
-piece on Mother Theresa. Calling her
just this calculating nun, exploiting
people's pain. *But this was before I'd heard*
the dead man speak to me. Either you'll die

in the streets, or you'll die in Mother's House,
and if you die in Mother's arms at least
someone was listening to you. Not because
they owe it to you, or because they feel
some familial obligation – they're just
listening because they know we all deserve
to be loved. Maybe I'm an idiot
but I think that's the point. Or the question,
you know?

The War Reporter Paul Watson Gives the Poet Some Advice

Hey, that thing you said about your family
locking the door behind you. Your father
howling, *There are things you do not know!* Cue
the slapstick of their retriever retching
on your shoes. Into the spongiform lawn.
Your brothers sped to their dreams. The stabbing
finger summoning poor old Lowell tumbling
his father through their heirloom clock. *I knocked
you down.* Or could've, anyway. Bowing
to the imaginary coronary. *And how
you look just like his brother – I can't stop
thinking about all that!* I remember
listening on the stairs. Grandma's depression
is sunlight in the voile. Mother's pleading
with God in the rafters. I know the man
isn't Him. Is he me? My uncle's face
bearded in the morning is a blessing
from a schizophrenic draft-dodger to
an unknown minor poet. He gives me
a children's Bible. No, he's giving you
something else. What's he given us before
he opens that locked door? *Why don't you start
asking some questions, Dan? That's what I'd do
if I were you.*

The War Reporter Paul Watson Also Hates Trucks

with names like Earthquake and Enola Gay
and Tundra and Titan and Sierra
Denali. Which is just Mount McKinley
for people who do yoga. Vortec V
-umpteen engines, tri-flex fuel systems with
hundreds of lbs.-ft. of torque. Wherever
that gets you exactly. Sounds nice. Satellite
radios. Blueteeth. LED TVs. Like
limousines! Who's driving these things? Russian
mobsters? Hip hop moguls? When I was young
let's say you were a farmer. Your pickup
truck looked like hell! all rust and dents and wall
-eyed headlamps. Exhausted tires. Tie-down cords
flogging the shoulder. Rubble, bushels, slabs
of sheetrock jounced skyward through windshields and
impaling innocents. At a red light
a mud-birthed pickup truck pulls up hauling
black-skinned corpses. Rolled in reed mats and stacked
in back, the cracked, dusted soles of their feet
sticking out like vaudeville damsels. More mud
and blood on frayed cuffs and hems. Machete
wounds a multitude of festering snouts. Look
again. And it's a pyramid of Persian
rugs, bagged and tagged in the glistening bed,
horns ululating. It's just a pet peeve,
I know, but something about these monster
American trucks drives me absolutely
around the bend.

The War Reporter Paul Watson Tells His Son a Story

East of Vancouver with my son walking
into the park at dusk. Barrier gates
lowering soon. Drizzle scurrying in. I joke,
What if we become trapped inside all night
with the wild beasts? with the cranes and the geese
and the cranky bears and lanky elk, minks
sneaking and oryx leaping, the lustful
yawling brawling dank vomitous lions
escaped from the zoo? My blood laughs. While rain
transcends into snow. Trembling maidenhead
ferns in their moss beds. We walk on. I joke,
What if all nature should stalk us and pounce
from that ridge above and in its dread jaws
snap poor Dad in half? what then? He laughs. Snow's
shoring up the lakeside of the girder
-like red cedar trunks. Hemlocks ecstatic
in their buffeting blast. The waves' abysmal,
numinous shudder. Steep switchbacks shredding
mud from his dear shoes to mine. What if men
are fingering icy branches? Fugitives
waiting for moonrise to slice their knives in
my soft side, then whirl around for you – what
then, my only son? He laughs. *I will fight*
them and if I can't defeat them I'll run
for the gate and I will escape because
I am small and fleet and innocent but
I promise I will always remember
a father as funny as you.

The Poet Gives the War Reporter Paul Watson an Excuse

The ghost's suit was torn and his briefcase fell
open. A pollen of cement and bone
ash. He looked so confused! Rising from bed
as sirens cycled closer and paper
statements spiraled down. *Now all the bankers
will be humbled.* Bought my latte in time
to see the second plane. An old woman
sat down on the crosswalk and started to
wail. As we walked away the working men
and women leapt. You know, I never saw
my brother throw himself out the window
of our attic. And sometimes I wonder,
Did it happen at all? A radio
on a stoop in Chinatown. A TV
in the sublet showed the second tower
collapse, while idiots tossed a Frisbee. Shocked
by the sameness of the light. Saw myself
aiming a submachine gun comically
in my mind's eye, someplace pure and barren
like Afghanistan, or maybe Iraq.
But I didn't go. Because I didn't
consider it the right war. Or because
no one made me.

The War Reporter Paul Watson Attends a Stoning

Two men stand accused of holding a knife
against a woman's neck and taking turns
raping her all afternoon in the bush.
Then stole her money, no more than 20
dollars US. Every cent from selling
this kind of leafy speed Somalis chew
to snuff out their hunger pains. The trial's
in a looted office. A hundred men
sitting Indian-style on a rug beneath
a ceiling of bullet holes. Bundled wire
dangling where lights used to be. Twelve judges
in leather dinette chairs fanned out behind
a secretary's desk. Every judge cradling
his Koran in his lap. Sweat anointing
elephantine foreheads. Watched over by
two boys with Kalashnikovs. One handling
his grenade loosely, eyelids flickering
in the heat. Both men confess. The victim
pursues from a corner the ephemeral
gazes of the guilty. One judge renders
the verdict through a megaphone, flogging
for the unmarried rapist, and stoning
to death the married one. The judge returns
the victim her money. Who thumbs her wad
of bills as the guards shepherd her rapists
into the shimmering square. Eddies of grit,
amputated statues of two veterans
of an unknown war raising their stone flag
into God's cyclone stare. The megaphone
summons our audience. The bachelor-rapist
is first, his T-shirt stripped off and secured

over his face. A judge counts off each blow
through the megaphone, as the guards take turns
whipping. The man writhing from each crack, welts
opening in crosses across the gleamed black
span of this back. Chanting, *There is no God*
in the world save Allah, and Mohammed
is his prophet. Every time he stumbles
and cries the crowd heckles him. Children laugh
and imitate his pratfalls. A hundred
lashes and now our rapist collapses
unconscious. Suspiciously silent men
drag his body down an alley to rouse
him with camel's milk. The married rapist
straightens, wrists released from ankles. Pleading
with the masked men walking past, insisting
he's not married. Who would rape somebody
if he already had a wife? The men
shred open a threadbare jute bag stuffed full
of broken concrete. The victim requests
she throw the first stone, but Sharia law
won't allow it. *I am happy because*
of what these two men did. Now the horror
of their torture will never die. The first
stone catches him behind the ear, scuttles
him sideways in the dirt like a fetus
and a cloudburst of stones erupts like hail
at first, then rocks the size of bread loaves and
our audience cheers an elderly man
lifting a perfect cinder block above
his head, then smashing it down where a gash
jackknifes the rapist's neck and the body

goes limp. Save for a foot that's quivering
like an echo falling silent. A guard steps
lightly, crow-like. And although the face
is mush, the rapist's chest shudders and spits
its bolus of blood. Don't make it too hard
for this man to die! The megaphone chides
even the most timid men. Continue
till it's over. No mercy! Ten minutes
and blood's a wellspring from the nose, swamping
the gored throat. Bruises and wounds powdered white
with concrete dust. Guards abandon the stained
stones where they rest against the fly-swept corpse
of the married rapist. *This is victory
for Mohammed. Take heed! you young women
who walk out in the sunlight embracing
young men – take heed!* The judges are angry
at what I still regret: Why did you not
take pictures? Because you wanted me to.
Because this time I did not want the world
to see.

The Poet Recognizes the War Reporter Paul Watson

slumped in his bed in the Arctic crying
like only snowfall. Also an icon
exuding olive oil. *Oh no not this*
familiar ghost again. He's my brother
slumped at the kitchen table. The morning
they brought him home from the hospital where
they'd taken away his shoelaces and
his belt. I stood in the doorway and watched
him eating ash. Why couldn't I sit down
and eat with him? Sorrow is the sickness
you catch if it doesn't catch you. I ran
outside to play with friends. *Are you hungry,*
Paul? They've left some dinner on the table
for us.

The War Reporter Paul Watson Listens to the Artist

I do mostly landscapes. Dog teams. I like
the silence. Here are two white bears fighting
over a seal? and I was just pounding
the ice into the paper. This one's called
"Spring Is Here." My father used to send me
outside to slide downhill on his sealskin
pelts. For fun, but also I'd be cleaning
away the blood. But I didn't know that
then! Ha ha ha. And then I drew this girl
in purple doing somersaults because
I wanted a sister. We were living
in igloos at the time. When an airplane
came down from the clouds and took me away
to Inuvik for school. They didn't say
nothing! Just took me. And I remember
being hit with things like rulers because
I didn't know how to speak their language
and going through all this other bullshit
I can't really talk about. I'm still mad
about it! Oh no, this picture isn't
a shaman picture, it's a picture of
throat singing. You know what that is? It's when
two women stand face to face on the ice
going *hum a heeya, ee um mum mum,*
hum a heeya, ee um mum mum until
one of us gets tired or passes out or
laughs, ha ha ha. I just drew this because
as an artist whatever speaks to you
you've got to put it down on paper, right?
But it's got nothing to do with shamans,
it's just art.

The Poet and the War Reporter Paul Watson Go for a Sled Ride

Outside, the Inuit hunter's beating
their muzzles with a stick. All tangled up
in frozen cord howling. A savage race
of idiot wolves. I sit like a raja
on a blue plastic tarp, my rubber boots
splayed above the ice above the sea with
the hunter's mouth behind my ear barking,
Gee! Gee! Zaw! The war reporter's clinging
to the skidoo driver's sides, red tail-lights
swerving in a whorl of snow. You feel it
in your spine, your neck, your skull, the grinding
of the rusted runners on ice crystals
like sand. Cresting invisible hillocks,
the dogs fan out to shit in streaks. We stop
where the ice runs out. The Arctic Ocean
like an undulating eternity
of inky slush a foot away. Seal heads
popping the newborn crust, their spectral eyes
on us. My feet are numb. My tailbone is
bruised, says Paul. Put your weight on this anchor,
says the hunter. Wait here while I go drain
my dragon. While the war reporter shoots
the skidoo driver discussing global
warming, as fat flakes hover and the dogs
are murderous. The steel anchor's just a claw
in the ice, tethered tautly to the cord
tethered to the craziest dog. *One time
I was trying to put my oinikhiot
in the water? after I'd hunted me
some seal? And my foot slipped in the ocean.
It's real dangerous, man. Real dangerous.* The sled

is escaping backwards, I'm laughing like
I'm ashamed, dogs rejoicing as my boot
slips off the anchor as the anchor slips
out of the ice and suddenly I see
the world as if from above. Hey Dan – Dan
are you okay? Because the anchor's wrapped
around my ankle and whipped me up off
my feet. *I'm so sorry, I'm so sorry*
I almost got you killed. But Paul I was
rejoicing, rejoicing as the seals ducked
back under the new ice.

The War Reporter Paul Watson Tries to Apologize to the Mother of the Dead

Flew to Phoenix. Um hello ma'am, yes. I
took that picture of your son that morning
in Mogadishu. Bright like Arizona
with the old man beating your son's chest with
a cane. That boy laughing at us. Driving
past strip malls and drive-thru drug stores, strip clubs
and plumbing supply. This is difficult
for me to tell you. Buzzed the gate. Slipping
through as someone else drove out. Stars and stripes
hanging limply off flag poles. Above-ground
pools, jet skis on cinder blocks. Your trailer
on a cracked patio, twin naked cherubs
blowing their horns. A lawn chair with beer cans
in the crab grass. Waiting all day for you
to come home. And I hope that you're willing
to give me a moment or two. I'm here
at the Ramada all weekend. Turning
on the AC, sliding blackout curtains
across. I know this will be hard for you
to hear, but I need to try and help you
understand.

The War Reporter Paul Watson is Forgiven

I'm going to have to ask you not to call
my mother anymore. Well sir it's just
I've been fighting this thing for years – You mean
that picture you took of my brother drug
through the streets? That's right, and I'm hoping if
I can just understand my place in time
and his place in time then maybe we could
bury a few things? He was just this kid
who didn't match in with nobody but
he always knew he wanted to protect
people. Was your father in the navy,
sir? He was an engine mechanic. And
did your brother have a wife? Well he had
a couple of them. And you wouldn't know how
I might go about trying to track down
these women, or other relatives? Nope.
He had a few kids I understand. What?
He had some children. Now are you looking
to do some kind of story again? Sir,
I just wish we could meet – I don't care to
meet you at all! Do you hate me? Sorry?
You hate me, I know it, sir. I don't hate
anybody, man! But I dishonored
your brother, that's what haunts me. His honor
wasn't tarnished in the least. Well, sir, see
a lot of people would argue with you
on that point. Then they must not've been one
of the 3,000 people that crowded
into the church that could hold only like
a hundred for his funeral, must not've
been one of the 32 cars following

us all the way to the cemetery,
or the four helicopters with gunships
giving him an escort from above, they
didn't feel he'd been dishonored. Others
who know him from my picture – I don't care
about your picture, I'm not interested
in discussing it, I'm not interested
in meeting you and I do apologize
if that offends you, sir! Could we do this
over email, sir? No. Can't we just meet
and you can see who I am? Once again
negative. Sir I have begged, I, I, I
don't understand why – You're going to have to
figure that out on your own. Your mother
hates me, sir, cause I read an interview
about what happened in Fallujah when
those American contractors got strung up
from a bridge? and your mom broke down and told
the reporter she hates the person who
did it then, just like she hates the people
who do it now. She was talking about
the people who were desecrating them
bodies. No, sir, she was talking about
me, sir, I know it! The thing of it was
we found out while watching Peter Jennings
when my mother recognized my brother's
feet, cause they looked just like his dad's. You must
blame me for that much! Man you don't listen
very well, do you? Do you want to know
why I did it? No. Why not? Explaining
don't change the fact a thing got done. The week

before, another Black Hawk got shot down
and kids were parading the body parts
of servicemen through the streets like pennants
at a baseball game, and the Pentagon
denied it, they said it didn't happen
because I didn't have a picture! Right.
I wasn't a machine, I cared! Right. And
honestly, sir, I believe your brother
would still be alive today if people
had known the truth. From my own life I'd say,
and I was in the Air Force for ten years,
I volunteered to go to Somalia
but they wouldn't let me, cause of my job,
where I was, and I can honestly say
I'd have no problem if I'd been the one
in my brother's shoes. You would've wanted
that picture taken? I would have. Why, sir?
for the reason I just explained? For both
reasons, what you just said and just because
you were doing your job. Well I'm grateful
to you for saying that. Not a problem.
It takes a weight off my back, but I wish
the rest of your family felt the same way.
You're going to have to take my word on that
unfortunately. Oh yeah no, I won't go
down that route, sir. I appreciate that, sir.
I'm just talking about the larger world
here, cause I don't think most people out there
understand. Well the world's fucked up. Yeah. Short
and sweet, the world's a fallen place. I hope
this won't upset you too much but one thing

that still haunts me is that I heard a voice
when I took that picture, and your brother
warned me, If you do this I will own you
forever. Well how do you know David
meant something bad? He said I will own you
forever – Maybe he meant you owe him
something now. Like what? Look, I've got to go
pick up my son. Okay sir, I forgot
to ask your name. Ray. Ray, that's my father's
name. Ha ha ha. Sir, please apologize
to your mother for me. Good night. Good night.

The War Reporter Paul Watson Invites the Poet

Apologies for not writing sooner
but the truth is I simply lost my grip
as we broke through a continent of ice
near Gjoa Haven. Watching as my camera
slipped out of my hand and into the wound
of the sea. I'm waiting here in Resolute
for this blizzard to clear so I can fly
tomorrow to Grise Fiord. All we have
is a Twin Otter on skis and because
our final approach is straight at a cliff
with a hairpin turn to land, the pilots
won't fly until it's windless. For one more
story about the Inuit people's
suffering, of course. But between me and you,
my confessor: the truth is I'm talking
to the *Star*. And how can I tell them no?
If I want to keep my wife and my son
in new snow boots I need to make myself
valuable again. And Canada's still
responsible for Kandahar. Truth is
I'm no different than all those Americans
driving convoy trucks in near-suicidal
conditions in Iraq, just to pay off
mortgages in Florida. This is what
I've turned into, a mercenary and
a desperate one at that. Just between me
and my confessor. But there's something else:
I think the ghost is glad I'm going back,
though I don't know why yet. Maybe you'll come
visit me? I have an old Afghan friend
who ran an English school in Kabul where

various Taliban factions would meet during the darkest days of this never -ending war on terror. And I'm thinking his story should be told. What do you say, my friend? I promise to keep you as safe as I can. Though of course nobody knows what will happen out here.

CB *editions*

Founded in 2007, CB editions publishes chiefly
short fiction (including work by Gabriel Josipovici,
Todd McEwen and David Markson) and poetry
(Fergus Allen, Andrew Elliott, Beverley Bie Brahic,
Nancy Gaffield, J. O. Morgan, D. Nurkse). Writers
published in translation include Apollinaire,
Andrzej Bursa, Joaquín Giannuzzi, Gert Hofmann
and Francis Ponge.

Books can be ordered from www.cbeditions.com.